LITTLE DID
WE KNOW

Financing the Trans Alaska Pipeline

To: Duane Collins

All the best
my friend!

by

JOHN R. MILLER

Published by John R. Miller, Arbordale LLC
37300 Fairmount Boulevard #5
Chagrin Falls, OH 44020
For more information, please contact office@johnrmiller.com or
440-247-2096.

Book design by Live Publishing Co.

Library of Congress Control Number 2012920814
ISBN 978-0-9885487-0-1

© 2012 by John R. Miller
First printing, December 2012

Printed in the United States of America

DEDICATION

This book is dedicated to Karen, my beautiful bride of more than fifty years, who managed the household and raised our children when I traveled and worked long hours; to my children, Rob, Lisa, and Jim, wonderful individuals of whom I am very proud; to their terrific spouses, respectively Mary, David, and Susan; and to my grandchildren, Grace Miller, Sam Turben, Mack Miller, Luke Turben, Caroline Miller, Jake Turben, and Christine Miller who are growing up rapidly, and by all indications, each and every one of them will make a positive contribution to society.

CONTENTS

FOREWORD

Fortune magazine published "For Sohio, It Was Alaskan Oil—Or Bust" in August 1977, a month after the Trans Alaska Pipeline (TAPS) started carrying crude oil 800 miles from the Prudhoe Bay field on the North Slope of Alaska to the ice-free port of Valdez on the southern coast of Alaska. The article covered The Standard Oil Company's involvement in the project, which was considered by many people, both inside and outside the oil industry, to be the greatest engineering marvel since the Panama Canal. It was the largest private industrial project ever undertaken, ultimately costing $8 billion. Including the cost of developing the oil field, the price tag for the entire project was $15 billion—roughly $65 billion in 2012 dollars.

Our decade-long effort to bring Alaskan oil to market transformed The Standard Oil Company (also known as Standard Oil of Ohio or Sohio) from a small, regional refiner and marketer short on crude oil to the third-biggest US producer and largest owner of domestic oil reserves. That transformation tells a remarkable story of surmounting challenges, not the least of which was securing the money to pay the company's share of the project's cost—something many seasoned finance practitioners thought was well beyond our capabilities.

The Fortune article's author states, "It is probably fair to say that seldom in the business of raising money have so few, who knew so little, done so much." I held primary responsibility for the money-raising, and I've always harbored mixed feelings about that statement—from being flattered to resentful, with a touch of amusement in between.

The author was correct about the number of people involved. At the outset, I had no staff, and over the life of the project, I added only three people. But the author's conclusion that we knew so little has always puzzled me. Perhaps she reached that conclusion because of my small-town background. I was born and raised in Lima, Ohio. Or my young age. I was 32 years old when Sohio's participation in the project began after a transaction with British Petroleum (BP) gave us ownership of BP's 53 percent interest in the Prudhoe Bay oil rim and, initially, a 27.5 percent interest in TAPS. Perhaps it was because my staff and I lacked formal training in finance. Maybe it was my small, "drab" (her words, not mine) office, or the fact that we were headquartered in the "fly-over" city of Cleveland, Ohio far removed from the centers of finance.

I'll grant the writer that there was a lot we didn't know. Little did we know that our share of the cost to build the pipeline, expected to be about $300 million at the outset of our negotiations with BP, would balloon to over $3.1 billion. Little did we know lawsuits by environmentalists would delay the start of construction by four years, and that Sohio would invest over $400 million in Alaska—more than the original estimate of our share of the cost to complete TAPS—before construction even began. Little did we know that our pipeline partners would decide ownership in TAPS would be in the form of an undivided joint interest. This structure, as opposed to a more conventional stock ownership, left each participant on its own to finance its share of TAPS, which exacerbated Sohio's mounting challenge. Little did we know the federal government's right-of-way permit would stipulate that the oil could not be exported, making it necessary to build, in accordance with federal regulations under the Jones Act legislation, six tankers to haul the oil from Valdez to the lower 48 states. Little did we know that Alaska would impose a tax on oil and gas reserves, adding $260 million to Sohio's costs. And little did we know that our investment in the project would end up being $6.3 billion, eight times the total assets of Sohio before our Alaskan venture began.

But, I don't think the author questioned our ability to divine the future. It was our financial know-how that was questioned. Little did the writer know.

My lack of formal finance training may have been a blessing in disguise. Sohio's chairman and chief executive officer during those times, Charlie Spahr, once noted, had I been trained in finance, I probably would have known that financing

Sohio's share of the cost of constructing the pipeline couldn't be done. Being somewhat ignorant in that regard, I set about doing it. Fact is, though, I did know a little something about finance. Years before our involvement in the Alaskan venture, I spent a summer working in Morgan Stanley's offices gaining an exposure to the fundamentals of finance. A wonderful experience, and the relationships I developed with the firm paid dividends later on. My responsibilities in Corporate Planning included analyzing the financial aspects of merger and acquisition opportunities. In addition to my "hands on" experience in finance, I had a background in planning that came in handy as I laid out our initial financial plan and then continuously revised it in an attempt to keep up with ever escalating costs and changing circumstances. The value of my experience and on-the-job training was apparently lost on the writer. But, perhaps most important, my father instilled in me a common sense approach to things. And I have a degree in chemical engineering from the University of Cincinnati where I was taught how to think and how to solve problems. Engineers are pragmatic, harnessing theory to practical use, and with that mindset I determined, at the outset of my financing adventure, which rules of finance were as incontrovertible as, say, the second law of thermodynamics (you can't pump heat uphill), and which ones were pliable, capable of being bent to serve our purposes. As you'll see, most of them fall in the latter category.

Did we succeed? No question. Excluding sales of commercial paper to provide interim financing, we raised $6.3 billion for the pipeline and oil field development. We raised another $325 million for non-TAPS related purposes during the same period, bringing the total dollars (mostly in the form of debt) swept into the company's coffers to almost $7 billion (about $30 billion in 2012 dollars). Our company had assets of only $773 million in 1969 when it all started. Although money got extremely tight at times, we avoided having to sell off portions of our Prudhoe Bay reserves in order to pay our bills, which would have been an extremely unfortunate turn of events for our shareholders. The year before we got involved in Alaska, Sohio's net income was

$73 million, and we were the 58th largest industrial corporation in the United States, in terms of assets. In 1980—the first full year of stable field and pipeline operations—our net income was $1.8 billion, and Sohio was the 15th largest US industrial corporation, by assets. After eight years of extensive investment to capitalize on the largest-ever oil field discovery in North America, tremendous value accrued to our shareholders.

What you will note in this narrative is that history repeats itself. This story of opportunity and challenge in the energy industry remains relevant. The United States still today lacks an energy policy and has made no meaningful progress toward its objective of energy independence. Environmental challenges that cause costly delays to projects aimed at producing domestic sources of energy, and therefore greater national security, continue to be the order of the day.

The dollar figures aren't as impressive today as they were when the story took place because of the ravages of inflation. To get a realistic perspective, multiply each figure by four or five. Also, we didn't have cell phones, personal computers, spreadsheets, PowerPoint presentations or other modern technologies that could have made our tasks easier. But then, we also didn't have the Transportation Security Administration, which was a good thing as you will see in the Divine Intervention chapter.

Finally, although I have undertaken extensive efforts to ensure accuracy, to some extent I've had to rely on my memory for pieces of the story. However, memory is imperfect in general, and mine is no exception, I'm sure. My apologies in advance for any mental lapses that may have occurred. And, out of consideration for the reader, I've avoided relating the excruciating detail and complexities of some of the financings, except when necessary to convey greater insight into the challenges we faced. And finally, this story is told from my perspective. Others familiar with events from their vantage point may differ with my accounting of things, but I hope such differences are small and, if reconciled, wouldn't change the message.

Please enjoy.

1. A TIGER BY THE TAIL

A funny thing happened as I was working diligently to get out of the Finance Department at Sohio and on to something more interesting. Events were taking place in the oil industry that would change Sohio's future in ways that none of us could have imagined. In March of 1968, Atlantic Richfield Company (ARCO) and Exxon (at that time the Humble Oil and Refining Company), two multi-billion-dollar oil companies, jointly drilled a discovery well in the Prudhoe Bay field located on the North Slope of Alaska.

British Petroleum (BP), owned in whole or in part by the British government until 1987, traces its origins to the Anglo-Persian Oil Company. Sir Winston Churchill, when he was first lord of the Admiralty, convinced his government to become a major shareholder of that company to provide a dedicated oil supply for the British Navy. BP, one of the largest oil companies in the world, had been exploring in Alaska since the 1950s, and had put together a land position comprised of leases from the state covering about 96,000 acres adjacent to where the ARCO/Exxon discovery well had been drilled. Shortly after the discovery well was announced, BP drilled a well on their leases nearby, which, together with the discovery well, confirmed that the Prudhoe Bay oil field was gigantic, by far the largest petroleum deposit ever found in North America. Petroleum engineers estimated that recoverable reserves contained in the main oil and gas reservoir amounted to about 9.5 billion barrels of crude oil and 24 trillion cubic feet of natural gas. Of those

2 | *Little Did We Know*

amounts, BP's leases were estimated to cover 5.1 billion barrels of oil and 7.1 trillion cubic feet of natural gas.

Upon hearing this, the executive team at Sohio, led by Charlie Spahr, Sohio's chairman and chief executive officer, felt it might be the company's last opportunity to achieve the corporate objective established in the mid-1960s: become self-sufficient in crude oil. The need for that objective was somewhat ironic, considering that we were the original Standard Oil Company, founded by John D. Rockefeller in Cleveland in 1870. Subsequently, we became part of the Standard Oil Trust, which was declared to be an oil monopoly under the Sherman Antitrust Act by the Supreme Court in 1911. The court ordered the trust to be broken up into 34 independent companies. As a result, we became a company separate from the others with properties only in Ohio and with the right to use the Standard Oil name only in the State of Ohio. Although we were still, as a legal entity, The Standard Oil Company, on occasion, we gratuitously added "Ohio" in parenthesis to distinguish ourselves from the plethora of other Standard Oils that were created, such as Standard Oil of New York (which became Socony and then became Mobil) and Standard Oil of Indiana (which became Amoco). We used Sohio as our brand name. We had no crude oil production of our own. From that modest rebirth, we became a successful marketer and refiner of petroleum products operating principally within Ohio. Although we managed to develop some crude oil production, it was consistently less than 30 percent of our refinery requirements.

Our long-range forecasts suggested that production of crude oil in the United States would peak in the early 1970s, and our ability to secure adequate supplies of our refineries' basic raw material thereafter would be highly problematic. Having to buy crude oil from our competitors when supplies were tight would put us in an untenable position and might threaten our survival. We had tried numerous tactics—an expanded exploration program, buying crude oil reserves in the ground, and acquiring one or more of the independent companies that had crude oil reserves—all to no avail. The best we were able to do was keep our precarious position from deteriorating any further. Until news of the Alaskan oil find, we had literally run out of ideas of how to improve this situation.

Charlie Spahr, select members of Sohio's management committee, which consisted of the top six executives of the company, and a few other subject matter experts within Sohio put their collective minds to finding a way to participate in the Alaskan discovery. A deal with Exxon or ARCO was out of the question for antitrust reasons. But BP was another story. For some time, it had harbored ambitions to expand its marketing and refining business into the United States. Now, with substantial reserves on the North Slope, the British oil company began seeking a partner that had domestic marketing and refining capabilities.

During World War II, the United Kingdom had implemented exchange controls in order to conserve the UK's gold and foreign exchange resources. The long and short of these controls was that they restricted foreign investment except where it had a positive impact on the UK's balance of payments. This made it difficult if not impossible for BP to finance the project on its own. So the domestic partner it was seeking also needed to provide the means to finance the cost of developing the Prudhoe Bay field and transporting the crude oil to market. Although a number of US oil companies fit BP's criteria, probably the only company that could pass muster with the Justice Department was Sohio.

This was a match made in heaven.

I don't know who approached whom, but highly confidential, tightly held conversations between a small group of top executives from the two companies commenced late in 1968. Sohio did not retain an investment banker for advice, and to the best of my knowledge, neither did BP, which was very unusual in a transaction of this magnitude. Executives from Sohio who participated in the negotiations were Charlie Spahr; Al Whitehouse, senior vice president and general counsel, who became president in 1970; Dick Sauer, executive vice president, who retired in 1970; John Ross, vice president, natural resources; and Paul Phillips, vice president, finance and planning. I worked on the deal in a sub rosa fashion, crunching numbers for Paul, who was my boss.

One fly in the ointment was the matter of a $100 million public debt offering that I had agreed with Paul to manage before I moved out of finance. More about Paul Phillips and my reluctance to stay in finance later. We had no sooner started work on the offering when discussions between Sohio and BP commenced. If we were to proceed with the offering, because of the material nature of the discussions, we would have to disclose the fact that negotiations were taking place—not something we were willing to do. Public knowledge of a possible deal between Sohio and BP could possibly stimulate action on the part of others to prevent it—competitors, for example, who might find it contrary to their interests.

That meant I had to call off the offering, but I couldn't reveal the real reason for doing so. I had to make something up, and there wasn't a whole lot that came to mind. Holding off until interest rates declined might do the trick. I fully realized that Rule Number One in finance (practitioners of the trade know that there are several Rule Number Ones, depending on circumstances) was that you don't play the market. That is, if you need the money, you go get it. You don't delay your offering, betting that either interest rates will come down or stock prices will rise, depending on whether you're selling debt or equity securities.

But playing the market was the best excuse I could come up with.

I called David Goodman, who oversaw our account at Morgan Stanley, to explain that it was my considered opinion that interest rates were going to come down, and therefore, it made perfectly good sense to delay the offering until we could get cheaper debt.

David must have wondered if I had learned anything at all during my internship in their offices a few years earlier. And besides, what did I know about interest rates. Without a doubt, I'm sure he thought I was clueless in that regard, to say nothing of arrogant and audacious.

David, not knowing the real reason for abandoning our offering, put forth arguments against the reason I gave, but obviously, his protests fell on deaf ears. My mission was clear: delay the offering. I listened for a reasonable period of time, and then I dismissed his arguments as not being persuasive. I concluded, "I have already convinced Sohio's management that delaying the offering is the right thing to do, and that's our position. I'll call you when we're ready to resume."

III

BP had an office in New York staffed by a team whose objective was to look at business opportunities in the United States. One such opportunity arose when ARCO acquired the Sinclair Oil Corporation. In order to get the Department of Justice's approval for the transaction, ARCO was required to divest itself of all of Sinclair's marketing properties in the sixteen Eastern seaboard states as well as two refineries; one in Marcus Hook, Pennsylvania and the other in Port Arthur, Texas. In April of 1969, BP acquired those assets from ARCO in exchange for a $400 million note, pledging its reserves in Alaska as collateral. That pledge was something that would give us a problem down the road.

In the course of our negotiations with BP—and true in most transactions—there were a number of potential "deal breakers" that had to be addressed. A couple of these loomed larger than the rest. First, our objective was to acquire BP's leases in the Prudhoe Bay field, nothing more. However, BP made it clear that its intention was to operate in the United States through a partner rather than conduct business here themselves. Consequently, as part of the deal, Sohio would have to acquire the Sinclair marketing, refining, and pipeline assets that BP had acquired from ARCO. Sinclair had a poor reputation as a marketer, selecting secondary sites for its service stations rather than paying up for good locations. As a result, the volume of gasoline sold through each outlet was generally insufficient to produce a profit. In addition to taking on assets that were almost certainly losing money, we knew it would take time and capital to turn the Sinclair properties around. We knew that capital was going to be a scarce resource for us, and therefore we did not want the Sinclair properties. BP held firm on its requirement, and we ultimately conceded the point, reluctantly agreeing to include the Sinclair assets in the deal.

The second sticking point in the negotiations revolved around the level of ownership in Sohio that BP would eventually obtain. From the outset, it was clear that buying BP's US assets outright wasn't a possibility for several reasons. First and foremost, BP didn't want to sell, preferring instead to exchange its Prudhoe Bay assets for an ownership position in Sohio in order to allow them to participate in the future rewards that would come out of the production of North Slope crude oil. Second, there was a lot of uncertainty about production rates from Prudhoe Bay and what oil prices were going to be over the its forty-year life, making it almost impossible to place a monetary value on the field that both parties agreed was fair. And finally, even if that had been possible, Sohio wasn't in a position to write a check anywhere near that size.

In short, Sohio stock, not cash, would be the currency of choice for the transaction.

But how much? To address this issue, the negotiating team came up with a very creative approach. In exchange for BP's assets, Sohio would issue BP "special stock" equivalent to a 25 percent common stock interest in Sohio. The special stock would have voting rights. However, it would not pay dividends until January 1, 1975, or production from Prudhoe Bay for Sohio's account reached 200,000 barrels per day, whichever came first, thus saving Sohio much needed cash until the field was up and running. Also, the percentage ownership of Sohio that the special stock would equate to would escalate in a step-wise fashion as Sohio's crude oil production from Prudhoe Bay increased until it reached 600,000 barrels per day. Production beyond that level would not earn BP any further stock interest in Sohio, but it would receive a 75 percent interest in the net profits from that production.

This was an elegant solution to a difficult problem until it came to establishing the ultimate ownership in Sohio that BP would earn. For obvious reasons, Sohio wanted it to top out at 49 percent. For equally obvious reasons, BP wanted it to top out somewhere over 50 percent. A good deal of haggling and hand wringing took place over that last one percent. Giving another company majority interest in Sohio was a major concession for us. But BP had something we desperately needed, and at the end of the day, we caved and agreed to a formula that would ultimately give BP ownership of about 53 percent of the company. After six months of hard bargaining, the terms of the deal were set, contingent on approval by the boards of directors of both companies, and then, by Sohio's shareholders.

Out of an abundance of caution and consistent with efforts to keep the negotiations secret, Charlie Spahr had not kept Sohio's board informed of the discussions with BP. He called a special board meeting for June 2, starting at lunch, and warned the directors that it would be a lengthy session. They were not told what was on the agenda. BP arranged for its board to meet at the same time. The presentation was scheduled to run until after the market closed, when, assuming board approval was obtained, press releases would be issued simultaneously in Cleveland and London. In keeping with the tight security measures that had been deployed throughout the negotiations, the Sohio directors were locked in the board room with no access to telephones (cell phones or blackberries would not come into existence until decades later) until the meeting was over.

The company had made incredible efforts over the six months of negotiations to keep the discussions secret for fear that any leak could damage the deal. There had been no unusual activity in the stock over the previous month, and if things went according to plan, we only had to maintain security for one more day. My boss, Paul, was going to be in meetings all day, including the board meeting, and he asked me to get a message to him immediately if it looked like word had gotten out and the stock was reacting to it. The internet didn't exist, so to get up-to-the-minute stock prices, you had to call a stock broker.

Along with my other finance duties, I had been given responsibility for investor relations. But I never got in the habit of calling anybody to check on our stock. It just wasn't volatile enough to bother with and the daily *Wall Street Journal* kept me sufficiently current. This meant that I needed to be careful, in calling around to check on Sohio's stock price, not to raise suspicions. I came up with the names of a few brokers around town that I could call for various innocuous reasons, and then get around to asking about Sohio's stock. I waited a decent interval after the market was scheduled to open, called a broker, and when I got around to asking nonchalantly how Sohio's stock was faring, I was told that it hadn't opened.

Panic set in. Had there been a leak that triggered an imbalance between buy and sell orders? Then, after an excruciating pause, the broker told me that storms in the Northeast had delayed the opening of the New York Stock Exchange. It wasn't until 10:45 a.m. that stocks began to trade that day.

After that initial panic, I spent the rest of the day periodically tracking the stock. Nothing unusual. We closed down ¾ of a point at $70¼ per share. I think it's fair to say that this was probably the only day in the company's history when management was happy the stock went down. Both boards approved the deal. The amalgamation—the term we used since technically, it was neither a merger nor an acquisition—was announced. The reaction in the marketplace was extremely favorable. The next day, the stock didn't open. The change in Sohio's prospects was so huge that, initially, prospective buyers and sellers of our stock had trouble coming to agreement on valuation. The bid-ask spread was so wide that the NYSE specialist handling Sohio's stock was unable to close it. On the following day, after buyers and sellers had time to digest the news, the stock finally opened above $95 per share, closing at $100, up more than 40 percent.

Up until now, the analysts that covered the oil industry essentially ignored Sohio. Our deal with BP changed all of that and, as the one responsible for investor relations, requests from me for information increased dramatically. Shortly after the transaction was announced, the analyst from Value Line who covered Sohio called looking for information.

Value Line published a notebook containing its investment research. Information on each company they covered was summarized on one page. Down in the lower right hand corner was a box showing their five-year projections for revenues and earnings. In order to fill out this box, the analyst wanted to know what our revenue projections were for the next five years, recognizing that the onset of production from our interests in the Prudhoe Bay field would materially increase our top line. From there, she could estimate the impact on our earnings.

Besides being information we didn't disclose, I told her with all of the uncertainties—pipeline capacity, production levels, crude oil prices, the accounting treatment to be adopted for our own usage of North Slope crude oil or swaps, etc.—it would be difficult to develop a forecast of revenues that Value Line would find worthy.

"Under the circumstances," I suggested, "perhaps you could forego filling in the box and, instead, focus your commentary on the value of our 5 billion barrels of recoverable reserves and the transformation that Sohio will undergo as a result."

"I'm required to fill in the box," she said. "No exceptions."

"I can give you some parameters," I said. "But the variances are so great, I don't think that would be of much help to you. Sorry"

Disgruntled, she hung up.

A week or so later, I received a copy of her research report. She had successfully solved her dilemma. For the projections required to fill out the box, she merely extrapolated from our current results for the next five years assuming there would be no revenues coming from Prudhoe Bay. In her commentary she explained that, although the BP transaction would be a transformational event for Sohio, development of the Prudhoe Bay field and the construction of the Trans Alaska Pipeline (TAPS)—huge projects—would most likely be delayed and it would be at least five or more years before the company would realize any benefits from it.

It was gratifying that, with this one exception, the investment community agreed with our perception of the transaction, which was, indeed, a unique opportunity and one that could transform the company from a, regional marketer and refiner light on crude oil into a major player in the oil industry. But a lot had to be done before we could declare victory. We were now responsible for funding the cost of developing our half of the Prudhoe Bay field and paying for our share of the cost of building the TAPS which, together, we estimated would cost us somewhere in the neighborhood of $500[1] million, a tremendous challenge for a company our size.

Motivated by the sheer magnitude of the challenge, I told Paul, contrary to my earlier comments about how boring finance was and my insistence that he find something more interesting for me to do, I was prepared to remain in finance. I thought I had a good appreciation for how tough it was going to be.

Little did I know.

---

[1] See Exhibit 2, Summary of Sohio's Alaskan Project Cost Estimates and Oil Prices, in center of book.

2. THE PLAN

The BP-Sohio deal was now out in the open and, while we worked to consummate it, we began planning to finance our Alaskan venture.

First, though, I had to take care of old business. I turned my attention to the $100 million financing that had been abruptly interrupted when negotiations began, the one I had delayed because, in my infinite wisdom, "interest rates were too high." To get Morgan Stanley geared up for the task, I called David Goodman and found him to be in good spirits for a couple of reasons. Not only did he now realize that Morgan Stanley's efforts to train me had not been a complete waste of time, but also that his client, Sohio, was going to need his firm's services more than ever.

From my perspective, I was delighted to have David as a resource and an ally. First and foremost, he was intelligent, creative and tenacious. David graduated from Yale with honors in History, Arts and Letters. Upon graduation, he enlisted in the Air Force where he learned to fly F-86L Sabre Jets, all-weather interceptors. From there, he joined Morgan Stanley as the firm's 115th employee since its inception in 1936, ultimately becoming a partner and managing director. Later, in the 1970s, when Robert H. B. Baldwin, Undersecretary of the United States Navy during the Vietnam War, became chairman of Morgan Stanley, David was among the group of young partners who helped fashion the firm's long-range strategic plan that set it along a path to becoming the behemoth that it is today. Clearly, David would be able to galvanize all of the resources within Morgan Stanley in support of our cause.

Preparations for the offering began and on July 10, 1969, we sold $100 million of 30-year debentures to the public with an interest rate of 7.6 percent.[2] Morgan Stanley and F.S. Moseley co-managed the underwriting, a very unusual arrangement for Morgan Stanley but one that fulfilled a promise we had made to Moseley, Sohio's former investment banker. This financing took care of the obligations that had needed funding prior to our deal with BP.

Now, Sohio was about to step into BP's shoes, and as soon as the transaction was finalized, Sohio would be responsible for paying what had been BP's share of the cost of developing the Prudhoe Bay field and constructing TAPS. BP brought us up to date on the status of both facets of the project, giving us a sound basis for developing the critical assumptions to be used in laying out our initial financial plan and forecast.

When our negotiations with BP began, the three owners of TAPS ... ARCO, BP and Exxon ... were equal partners. But then, early in 1969, the partners agreed to a change in ownership. Exxon reduced its participation to 25 percent and ARCO and BP both raised theirs to 37.5 percent, thereby increasing Sohio's share of the cost of building the pipeline.

Preliminary feasibility studies, conducted by a task force made up of engineers from the three owners, had determined that the pipeline would have an initial capacity of 500,000 barrels per day, rising to 1.2 million barrels in 1975 and 2 million barrels per day in 1980. To accommodate this, TAPS would need to be 48 inches in diameter. The pipeline would run 800 miles from the North Slope to the ice-free port of Valdez on the southern coast of Alaska. From there, tankers would transport the crude oil through Prince William Sound and the Bay of Alaska to the Pacific Ocean and on to its ultimate port of destination.

The proposed route of the pipeline would cross some of the most rugged terrain in North America. Conditions that the engineers designing the pipeline had to take into account were extreme. Temperatures along the route ranged from

---

[2] See Exhibit 1, Sohio Alaskan Project Financings, in center of book.

90 degrees Fahrenheit in the summer to minus 80 degrees Fahrenheit in the winter. The idea of allowing the oil to cool—it comes out of the ground well above 100 degrees Fahrenheit—and then shipping it had been dismissed for both technical and cost reasons in favor of shipping the oil hot. However, much of the pipeline would traverse permanently frozen rock and soil, called permafrost, and shipping the oil hot would present its own set of technical challenges. Burying the pipeline, the conventional mode of construction, in those areas where permafrost existed risked melting it and causing serious damage to the environment.

Further, the pipeline would cross one major earthquake zone, three major mountain ranges, reaching its highest elevation of 4,800 feet at Dietrich Pass in the Brooks Range, and more than 500 rivers and streams, 34 of which were classified as major. Adding to the challenge, there were no bridges across the Yukon River and there were no roads north of the Yukon. New roads and bridges would have to be built to get construction equipment positioned along the pipeline's route.

Requests for Federal and State rights-of-way permits had been filed in June of 1969 and, supposedly, permission to start construction would be granted expeditiously. Work on a supply road north of the Yukon would begin later in the summer of 1969. Pipeline construction would begin in earnest in 1970 and would take about two and one-half years to complete, with startup scheduled for sometime in 1972. However, our chairman, Charlie Spahr, who had been involved with construction of the China-Burma-India pipeline, the longest of its type in the world built to provide fuel to the front lines in Burma and China during World War II, felt that the hostile conditions that would be faced in the course of constructing TAPS were so formidable that delays would be inevitable and he instructed us, for financial planning purposes, to assume startup would take place sometime in 1973.

From a financial perspective, the total cost to build the pipeline was estimated to be approximately $900 million and, Sohio's share of the cost would be around $300 million. Plans for developing the Prudhoe Bay field were also underway and it was estimated that Sohio would need to invest close to $200 million prior to the startup of TAPS to develop its half of the field. Crude oil was selling for a little more than $3 a barrel and, the assumption was, it would stay at that level throughout the planning period.

With the economic assumptions set, next came the task of devising a strategy for raising the substantial sums that would be needed for our Alaskan project. Since the funds that Sohio's operations would generate during the construction period were somewhat anemic relative to the projected needs, the question of how to secure funding from external sources loomed large.

One of the saving graces in terms of how much money we needed to raise was that pipelines were frequently organized as stand-alone companies. Under that arrangement, each of the owners of the pipeline would, typically, contribute 20 percent of their proportionate share of the cost of building the pipeline as equity, or stock ownership, in the standalone company. The pipeline company itself would then borrow the remaining 80 percent of the cost of construction. As security for that debt, each of the owners would enter into a throughput agreement with the pipeline company and its lenders guaranteeing that the owner would either ship enough crude oil or product through the pipeline to enable the pipeline company to generate enough cash to service that owner's proportionate share of the pipeline company's debt or, failing that, would pay the pipeline entity sufficient funds to enable it do so.

The beauty of that form of pipeline ownership is twofold. First, the throughput undertaking is a contingent liability and is not required by General Accepted Accounting Principles (GAAP) to be recorded as a liability on the owner company's balance sheet. Second, by introducing a high level of debt into the pipeline company's capital structure, the cost of financing the pipeline is reduced because debt is a cheaper source of funds than equity. Bottom line, or so we thought at the time, we only needed to come up with 20 percent of our share of the cost of building TAPS. Although we still needed to raise the funds to pay for our share of the cost of developing Prudhoe Bay, using the conventional mode of ownership of TAPS would significantly reduce the amount of external financing that we would otherwise have to do.

As a planner, I was always mindful of the poet Robert Burns's observation that "the best laid plans of mice and men oft times go astray." Or, in today's vernacular, "stuff happens." Or words to that effect. Consequently, as a matter of course, I routinely reviewed my rationale for the premises I used in formulating my plans and then reworked them if events took place that rendered my plans unrealistic or infeasible. Events that occurred during the last half of 1969 that would shape Sohio's destiny—some good, some bad and some indifferent—drove Burns's admonition home to me in spades. No doubt, we were in for a wild ride.

First, the good news.

After the Prudhoe Bay discovery was announced, other oil companies began to explore on the North Slope with a modest degree of success. Although their potential production was small compared to Prudhoe Bay, a number of them were interested in vertical integration via an ownership position in TAPS. In August of 1969, ARCO and BP each reduced their share of TAPS from 37.5 percent to 27.5 percent to make room for five new owners who, collectively, took up the 20 percent. That realignment would reduce our ownership in TAPS once we traded places with BP, with a corresponding reduction in our share of the construction costs.

Although construction of TAPS hadn't started, progress was being made in the horrendous task of marshaling supplies. In September, the first shipload of pipe from Japan arrived in Alaska. Since laying our hands on 800 miles of 48-inch pipe in a timely fashion was one of the items on the critical path, this was a welcome harbinger of good things to come. Or so we thought.

As exploration successes continued on the North Slope, the State of Alaska decided to take advantage of the oil companies' appetite for more leases to explore and, on September 10th of 1969, they auctioned off 164 tracts for a total of $900 million. To the chagrin of the winning bidders, neither Sohio nor BP bid, knowing that the geology of the leases being offered for sale was such that the prospects of discovering oil there was not particularly good. This event, while newsworthy, didn't register at the time as one that would have any impact on Sohio. But, as we would find out later, it did.

Now the bad.

Shortly after our deal with BP was announced, the DOJ attacked the transaction on the basis that it would eliminate "potential" competition. For years, BP had made known its desire to penetrate the gasoline market at the retail level throughout the United States. Citing BP's ambitions and predicating their decision on the "Clorox" case, the DOJ indicated that the proposed merger eliminated potential—not actual—competition and Sohio would have to reduce its sales of gasoline in order to get their approval.

The Clorox case was one where actual competition between Clorox and its acquisition target didn't exist. But, the DOJ believed that, absent the acquisition, Clorox would enter the business it was trying to acquire, so it deemed the merger anti-competitive. The department felt the same was true in our case.

In negotiations that followed, the DOJ insisted that Sohio divest itself, by sale or exchange, of 400 million gallons of annual retail gasoline sales in the State of Ohio as well as either our service stations in Western Pennsylvania or the stations that BP had acquired from ARCO that were located there. This precondition was a very difficult one for Sohio to accept. Being crude oil deficient, our historic profitability was highly dependent on our refining and marketing segments, and we were the premier marketer of gasoline in Ohio, having about a one-third share of the market. This demand was something that gave senior management considerable cause to pause.

As management was mulling over the DOJ's demands, the second issue of the latter half of 1969 hit us. In December, the National Environmental Policy Act (NEPA), a sweeping change in America's policy with regard to the environment, was enacted. This act required all federal agencies to publish environmental impact statements before taking any action likely to have a significant effect upon the environment. Shortly after the passage of NEPA, a number of environmental groups joined forces and filed a lawsuit claiming that the owners of TAPS had not complied with NEPA and, furthermore, that their permit application had requested the grant of a right-of-way across Federal lands in Alaska in excess of what was authorized by the Mineral Leasing Act of 1920. The Secretary of the Interior was subsequently enjoined from granting TAPS the federal permits it had requested until these environmental and right-of-way issues were addressed.

The final element in the 1969 negative hat trick was that in December, the TAPS task force updated their cost estimates for the pipeline taking into account the need to build a permanent road north of the Yukon and adding further environmental safeguards. The new estimate was $1.3 billion, up almost 50 percent from the initial estimate and more than offsetting the savings that we expected by virtue of our reduced ownership.

As 1969 was coming to a close, Sohio faced a couple of serious obstacles standing in the way of bringing its Alaskan venture to fruition. It would be necessary to agree to a significant reduction in our retail sales of gasoline in order to move forward with our transaction with BP. There was no federal permit to build a pipeline, and with NEPA the new order of the day, a lot of uncertainty was introduced into the permitting process. And, to make matters worse, the costs of constructing TAPS had increased by 50 percent!

After a good deal of angst, Sohio's management concluded that, despite the demands imposed by the DOJ, the strategic and economic benefits to Sohio of our deal with BP were compelling and we finally acceded to DOJ's demands. A consent decree to that effect was entered into on December 1, 1969. That hurdle was the last one standing in the way of our amalgamation with BP and we closed on January 1, 1970. With that historic event behind us, I began laying the groundwork for financing the ever escalating costs of Sohio's Alaskan venture.

3. Engineering It Is

Before going forward with the story, some personal background for perspective. I was an engineer by training and never harbored any ambition to get into finance. I was born and raised in Lima, Ohio, population 75,000, an industrial town in the state's northwestern corner, roughly situated between Toledo and Dayton, surrounded by farmland and smaller, rural communities. I had an older brother, Jim, and a younger sister, Ann. Mom was a nurse-turned-housewife. Dad was a school teacher, principal of an elementary school and a strict disciplinarian. Both of my parents were raised on farms.

In the 1950s, teachers worked for starvation wages: my father had to work at odd jobs to make ends meet. Despite the family's financial condition, he insisted that each of us get a college education. Knowing the strain that my college education would put on the family budget, I decided to try to pay my own way. I got my first job at age thirteen, scrubbing floors at a local bakery making sixty-five cents an hour. The next two summers, I was fortunate to land a job as a draftsman for an electrical contractor, making $1.50 an hour. A mild recession in the following year eliminated that job, and the best employment I could find was work at my neighbor's grocery store in a bad part of town making thirty-five cents an hour. Fortunately, I was able to work a lot of hours, which partially made up for my paltry wages. Altogether, my summer jobs enabled me to save enough to pay for my first year of college.

I did not want to follow in Dad's footsteps, career-wise. I preferred something more lucrative. I was good in math and science, and so my counselors suggested I give engineering a try. DuPont was running TV ads showing chemistry labs with a labyrinth of glassware through which brightly colored liquids bubbled and using the tagline, "Better living through chemistry." Somewhat fascinated by this, I decided to study chemical engineering. Although I didn't have a clue what chemical engineers did, I understood they were paid reasonably well.

Having settled on a course of study, the next hurdle was selecting a college. Because we couldn't afford to take trips to check them out, my selection process consisted of browsing through college catalogs, not visiting them. I came across Purdue University and, thinking it met my criteria I decided to apply, but found that it required a $25 application fee. Talking this over with my father, he suggested that I ignore Purdue because none of the other schools I was interested in charged an application fee. However, having amassed the princely sum of $1,500, enough to see me through my freshman year, to say nothing of laying out $25, I decided to send in my application. Shortly thereafter, I received word that not only had I been accepted, but I had been granted a four-year scholarship that paid the additional tuition charged to out-of-state students. I showed this to my dad, noting the handsome return I had made on my $25 investment, and dashed off my acceptance letter to Purdue.

But, Standard Oil muddied the water. I was summoned to the principal's office along with several of my classmates, where we were introduced to the manager of Human Resources at Sohio's Lima Refinery, Charles H. King III. Mr. King had asked to meet with students who were planning to study chemical engineering, looking for two who might be interested in attending the University of Cincinnati. UC had a cooperative education program whereby students alternated classroom time with work sessions in their field of study, and Mr. King wanted to initiate a program for co-op students at the refinery as a recruiting tool for chemical engineers.

Because of the co-op program, it took five years to finish chemical engineering at University of Cincinnati versus four elsewhere. But chances were good that I could pay my own way through school with my co-op job, relieving my father of that burden. I let Standard Oil know I was interested. A couple of weeks later, I spent a Saturday at the refinery, taking a battery of tests along with a number of others who were vying for the same opportunity. Shortly thereafter, I was told the job was mine. I accepted, and with Standard Oil's help, I enrolled in the University of Cincinnati. My father observed that Standard Oil had a good reputation as a place to work, and UC's engineering school was highly rated.

"All in all," he said, "a good move. Now, tell me again about the $25 you sent to Purdue."

That was vintage Dad. Imbued with a good deal of common sense and very practical—traits I attributed to his upbringing on the farm. I've always admired how self-reliant farmers are. My father was that way and I marveled at times at his simple, basic approach to getting things done. One example: he decided to build a small patio in our backyard. Having had some surveying experience on my co-op job, I told him I could probably borrow a transit from the refinery and use it to make sure that the patio was laid out properly and that the corners would be perfectly square. He asked me if I had ever heard of the Pythagorean Theorem, which of course I had. (In a right triangle, the square of the hypotenuse is equal to the sum of the squares of the two sides.)

"Well then," he went on to explain, "if you take three pieces of string that are three feet, four feet and five feet in length and attach them to three stakes, they'll form a perfect right angle."

So much for my hi-tech solution. I think I inherited my dad's pragmatism and perhaps that stoked my interest in engineering.

Starting in September 1955, I spent the next five years rotating between my studies at UC and my co-op job at Lima Refinery. Upon graduation, Standard Oil offered me a job in the long-range facilities planning group in the Engineering Department at its headquarters in Cleveland, Ohio. I accepted, believing that I was launching a life-long career with Sohio in the field of engineering.

Little did I know.

The author on assignment in the metal inspection department during a shutdown at Sohio's Lima refinery. He pursued a degree in chemical engineering at the University of Cincinnati in a cooperative education program whereby students alternated classroom time with work sessions in their field of study.

4. RATING AGENCIES

To attract the funds required to pay for Sohio's share of pipeline construction and field development, it was highly desirable, if not absolutely essential, to maintain at least a single "A" rating on our debt from Moody's and Standard & Poor's (S&P). Many institutional investors—pension funds and the like—could not buy lower-rated securities. Considering these ratings would play an important role in our financing efforts, I endeavored to completely understand the metrics these two rating agencies used to assess a company's creditworthiness. While the agencies were less than transparent about how they arrived at their conclusions, a few things were known. For instance, it was pretty well accepted that a debt-to-capital ratio of 35 percent was the upper limit beyond which a company risked losing its single "A" rating. We were going to exceed that debt threshold by a wide margin, even early on when the estimate for our Alaskan project was in the neighborhood of only $500 million. And we knew almost assuredly that we would come up short on various other ratios and factors used by the agencies to rate securities. A novel approach would be needed and my experiences outside of finance would come in handy.

As a chemical engineer, I was taught to adapt scientific principles to a useful end. Some principles, such as the second law of thermodynamics, are incontrovertible while others produce theoretical answers that need to be adjusted in order to get desired results. If you design a process that pumps heat uphill in violation of the second law of thermodynamics, it won't work. On the other hand, for example, if you use a McCabe-Thiele diagram to determine the number of theoretical trays needed to get a desired fractionation, unless you apply empirical relationships to convert to the number of trays that are needed in the real world, your distillation tower won't work. Understanding that there may be a difference between theory and practice was a valuable insight.

Another experience that proved useful was the time spent conducting operations planning for Sohio's five refinery system using linear programming. Simply stated, a linear program is a series of simultaneous equations that defines your system—what resources or capabilities are available and what constraints exist. Then, within that "operating space" an algorithm selects the optimum answer from among a number of possible solutions. And, the program indicates for each resource how much value there is in providing more of it and for each constraint how much it's worth to loosen the restriction. After a while, I began to think like a linear program in a general way, putting the emphasis on those things that give you the most bang for the buck in terms of the expenditure of one's time and energy.

A dear colleague of mine—Jim Stover who was Chairman and CEO of Eaton Corporation—used to say that "you are what you were when." In other words, we're all shaped by our life experiences. As a newcomer in the field of finance, I drew on my engineering and planning background—that mindset—to gain the in-depth understanding that I was looking for. Which laws or rules of finance are not open to question and which ones are pliable, capable of being bent to serve one's purpose? What defines the operating space that one has? Which constraints are rigid and which can be expanded to provide a little extra room? And what has the highest priority? Over time I learned that there was a good deal more flexibility than conventional wisdom would have you believe. Even GAAP proved not to be as ironclad as I initially thought as alternative ways of booking things were available to us. We pushed the envelope, but always within the bounds of propriety.

Our first test with the agencies came in late 1969 when we asked them to rate the debentures we planned to offer in January 1970. I began working with David Goodman, leaning heavily on his creativity, to develop a presentation that would cast our situation in a favorable light. One thing worked against us: GAAP limited the value of our Prudhoe Bay reserves that we could carry on our balance sheet to our costs of that asset, which was small relative to the true worth of our 5 billion barrels of oil. To overcome this, we provided illustrations that showed how the strength of our balance sheet would improve dramatically if the true value of our reserves was factored into the analysis. And, using the concept of project financing—David's idea—we prepared projections designed to demonstrate that our Alaskan venture made economic good sense. Project financing is based upon the projected cash flows of the project rather than the balance sheets of the project's sponsors. As such, it put the focus on the merits of our Alaskan venture rather than Sohio's anemic financial condition.

Project financing would be our story and we planned to stick to it.

Our first meeting was with Albert Esokait, an elderly gentleman who headed Moody's bond rating service. Moody's had rated Sohio's previous bond issues "AA," the second highest rating tier you could get after AAA and we hoped to retain that rating. David, Paul Phillips, and I attended the meeting, and we earnestly made our case.

A few days after the meeting, Mr. Esokait phoned David with his conclusion: he was concerned about the magnitude of the undertaking and all the uncertainties it entailed. He felt the project likely would take longer than we thought it would. He believed that the cost would be higher than we forecasted. He wanted to issue us a rating he could stick with through the duration of the project because he felt downgrading our rating later would be unfair to investors that came in early in the project.

So he dropped us to single "A." I was a bit irritated but, quite frankly, I had failed to see just how wise and prophetic Mr. Esokait was.

The same day of our Moody's meeting, we visited Russ Fraser, who was in charge of bond ratings at S&P. Like Moody's, S&P had rated our debt "AA." Russ, considerably younger than Mr. Esokait, had been trained to impute a dime-a-barrel value for domestic oil reserves when evaluating creditworthiness. That added roughly $500 million of assets to our balance sheet. It was obvious from Russ's body language that he saw the project as a great, albeit challenging, opportunity for Sohio. He confirmed this by maintaining our "AA" rating.

With our ratings established, we sold $150 million of 30-year debentures yielding 8½ percent to the public, with the proceeds to be used for constructing the pipeline.

1970 was just beginning. Our Washington colleagues informed us that the federal right-of-way permits should be forthcoming in a matter of weeks. Money from our first TAPS financing was in the bank. 1970 was starting off much better than the year just ended. The project that would transform Sohio was underway.

Little did we know.

5. WE COME CROSS BIG WATER IN SILVER BIRD

Not a single US steel company had a mill that could make the pipe.

The specs were difficult. It had to meet the special characteristics metallurgists felt were necessary for the harsh conditions to which the pipeline would be subjected. In addition to withstanding extremely low temperatures, it needed to be sufficiently ductile to expand and contract across wide swings in temperature without being permanently deformed. The walls needed to be thick enough to withstand pressures up to 70,000 pounds per square inch to deal effectively with elevation differentials encountered in crossing three major mountain ranges. Two thicknesses were specified: 0.462 inches and 0.562 inches. Perhaps the toughest specification of all was the diameter: 48 inches. No US steel company could roll 48-inch pipe.

Delivery was an issue too, because getting the pipe to Alaska and then distributing it along the pipeline route was going to be a logistical challenge, considering restrictions on transporting anything over permafrost and tundra, fragile terrain that was highly protected from an environmental standpoint. Plans were to start construction as soon as the weather improved in the spring of 1970, which meant the pipe needed to start arriving in Alaska well ahead of that.

In early 1969, the pipeline owners solicited bids from pipe manufacturers in the United States, Europe, and Japan, but only a consortium of Japanese steel companies could meet both the tough technical specifications and the delivery schedule. In fact, to meet the delivery schedule, it was going to be necessary for them to increase mill capacity. They submitted a bid of $100 million, and Exxon, ARCO, and BP began negotiating the details of a contract. There was no doubt that constructing the pipeline was going to be an expensive proposition and the owners were looking to use every conceivable means of financing it. Supplier credit was a real possibility in that regard, and one of the provisions that the pipeline owners were bargaining hard for was extended payments rather than cash on delivery, the terms preferred by the Japanese. Finding a way to provide credit that was satisfactory to both sides proved difficult, and over time, all of the other terms and conditions of the contract were agreed upon except how we would pay for the pipe.

Late in April, while negotiations were still in progress, the TAPS owners got wind of legislation that Representative Wilbur Mills (D-AR), the powerful chairman of the House Ways and Means Committee, was planning to introduce. This was before the public's awareness of Mill's penchant for fast women and hard liquor, which surfaced a few years later when the US Park Police stopped Mills in his car late at night near the Washington Monument. He was inebriated, and in the car with him was a stripper from Argentina who had the stage name of Fanne Foxe. Fanne jumped out of the car and ran into the tidal basin in front of the Washington Monument in an attempt to escape, but to no avail. Mills actually managed to survive this salacious public scandal, but another incident a couple of months later involving a drunken press conference from Fanne's dressing room did him in. He stepped down from his chairmanship, joined AA, and checked into rehab.

But at the time of interest to us, Congressman Mills was planning to introduce the Tax Reform Act of 1969 on the following Monday, legislation that would eliminate the investment tax credit we were counting on. This feature of the Internal Revenue Code, enacted to stimulate the economy, gave companies a tax credit of seven percent of their capital investments in plant and equipment. The effective date of legislation typically coincides with the date it is introduced. Knowing this, and fearful of losing the tax credit on a $100-million investment, the owners hastily signed the contract for the purchase of the pipe over the weekend, thus predating the presumed effective date of the tax credit's elimination. To deal with the payment issue, a clause was inserted in the contract that said, effectively, the Japanese consortium would offer the buyers credit on terms "to be negotiated."

There were two major stumbling blocks to agreeing with the Japanese on the matter of credit. First, although the Japanese would accept US dollars as payment for the pipe concurrent with its delivery, if payments were to be delayed for a number of years through the extension of credit, they insisted that payments be made in yen, not dollars. Conventional wisdom was that the yen would strengthen versus the dollar, so this provision was unacceptable to the owners because it would almost certainly raise the effective cost of the pipe, making the financing very expensive. Second, the Japanese wanted the buyers to cross-guarantee each other's obligations under the credit agreement. This feature was common practice in Japan, but not in America. For each of the owners to take on the liability for the cost of all of the pipe rather than their proportionate share was a non-starter for the owners.

Both sides were dug in, and negotiations between the owners and the pipe manufacturers' representatives located in the States continued for months with no progress. The fact that the representatives weren't authorized to make concessions didn't help. They merely served as go-betweens, transmitting the owners' positions to the powers-that-be back in Tokyo, and then communicating the response—"No"—back to the owners.

Finally, the higher-ups at Exxon, ARCO, and BP determined that the only way to break the logjam was for the owners to go to Tokyo and meet face-to-face with the executives from the manufacturers' consortium.

By the time that decision was made, we had stepped into BP's shoes. BP brought us up to speed on the issue and said it would be necessary for me to go to Japan, along with representatives from ARCO and Exxon, to continue the negotiations. I was also told in no uncertain terms that we had to be extremely careful not to do or say anything during the course of our negotiations that would cause the Japanese to slow down the production of pipe because it was on the critical path and nobody else had the capability to manufacture it.

Hearing that no progress had been made during months of negotiations on the two sticking points, and lacking negotiating leverage to use on the Japanese, such as, "if you don't make the concessions that we're asking for, we'll cancel the contract," I was convinced that traveling to Tokyo was a complete waste of time and shareholder money.

"Let ARCO and Exxon go," I said, "and if they're successful,"—which was highly doubtful—"we'll benefit, as well."

No soap. BP was adamant that we be represented. And their adamancy trumped mine. So, I got my shots and off I went.

ARCO's representative for the negotiations was its treasurer, Claude Goldsmith. Exxon sent Sequoia "Squaw" Brown, an Oklahoman and a senior financial executive in Humble Pipeline, the company's subsidiary that held its interest in TAPS. To give us time to get over our jet lag, we agreed to start our negotiations on the second day after our arrival, using the first day instead to visit Exxon's Tokyo offices to get a quick course in how to deal with the Japanese. On the cab ride over, Squaw sat in the passenger seat up front and I discovered that he had an unusual habit. Whenever he spoke to the Japanese cab driver, he broke down into—for lack of a better way to describe it—pidgin English. Odd, but I didn't think much about it at the time. Some people talk slower and louder in their native tongue when they encounter difficulties speaking with foreigners, and I just assumed this was Squaw's variation on that technique for communicating with someone who spoke a different language.

The time came to engage with the executives from the consortium. There were about fifteen of them. We started with the ritual of bowing and exchanging business cards, which was a big deal with the Japanese. During this process, all of the younger Japanese executives spoke English well, and I was willing to bet that most of them graduated from Harvard Business School. Introductions over, we took seats on opposite sides of a fairly large table, ready to get down to some serious bargaining. Squaw was the eldest among us, so Claude and I decided he would be our lead spokesperson. He sat between us.

When everybody was settled in, Squaw opened by making a sweeping gesture with his right arm, announcing that, "We come cross big water in silver bird."

Having come into the negotiations thinking we had a snowball's chance in hell, I now was convinced I had been overly optimistic about our prospects.

Recovering somewhat from Squaw's opening gambit, we spent the next week or so negotiating the two major obstacles to an agreement. We started with what we thought would be the easier of the two—their insistence that each of the owners guarantee payment of all of the debt, not just their own share. They gave us two reasons for taking this position. First, they did this all of the time, and they thought we were reluctant to do so because we didn't trust each other. And if we didn't trust each other, why should they? Second, having analyzed our financial statements, they thought a cross-guarantee was essential to provide adequate security for their loan to us. We took them through the way we would have to account for this cross-guarantee under US accounting standards, illustrating how it would unduly inflate our liabilities. Then we asked how they had concluded, absent the cross-guarantee, they would have inadequate protection.

I was worried that their concern might have been with Sohio's financial condition, as we were the weakest credit of the three owners. But to my surprise, they had concerns about all three of us. So taking Exxon, which among us clearly had the strongest balance sheet, as an example, we asked them to walk us through their analysis. It wasn't long before we realized they had missed the notation in parentheses on Exxon's financial statements—"thousands of dollars"—and failed to realize that they had to add three zeroes to get the numbers right. When we pointed this out, they conceded that it wouldn't be necessary for us to provide cross-guarantees.

To some extent, I think they caved out of embarrassment, but I also think this was a "throw away" because they were not going to give in on the second obstacle—denominating the obligations in yen. Both sides had valid reasons for their positions on the currency issue, making it difficult to find a resolution. We came at it from a variety of ways. The Japanese executives would listen politely and then would say they understood, but they couldn't agree without approval from the Ministry of International Trade and Industry. MITI was one of the most powerful agencies of the government, responsible for Japanese industrial policy, funding research, and directing investments. When we would reconvene the next morning, the Japanese would report that, unfortunately, MITI said, "No." Similar to what the negotiators back in the States had experienced months and months ago, we were negotiating with individuals who had no authority, or so they said.

After a week and a half in Tokyo, dying for a good cheeseburger, I told Squaw and Claude that I felt it was time to call it quits and go home. They had come to the same conclusion. I packed up and left, hoping my failure to bring home a victory would not be perceived as a self-fulfilling prophecy.

6. Computers Come of Age

A fter graduating from the University of Cincinnati as a chemical engineer, my initial assignment at Sohio was in the long-range facilities planning group. I was never one for career planning. Career-wise, my primary interest was in having a job that was interesting and challenging. There were a lot of opportunities for advancement at Sohio, both inside and outside of engineering, and I felt if I performed well, I would be given assignments of increasing importance as time went by. The fact that I spent a number of years later on in a key role in finance might seem strange on the surface, but I got there in a step-wise fashion, and every reassignment along the way made perfectly good sense.

My initial assignment in facilities planning was to evaluate capital investments that could lead to processing improvements at our refineries. Personal computers and spreadsheet programs did not yet exist, so we generated by hand—with the assistance of god-awful slow mechanical calculators—comparative cases reflecting system-wide refinery operations with and without the processing improvements under study. We knew enough about refinery economics to make adjustments in operating conditions that took into account seasonal differences in our product mix—maximizing gasoline production in the summer and furnace oil in the winter when the demand for those two major products was highest. But to determine optimal operating conditions, one would have to calculate the economics of every conceivable set of conditions and then select the one that yielded the best answer. Given all of the variables in a five-refinery system, that would require running hundreds if not thousands of cases by hand! It simply wasn't possible, which meant we could never be absolutely sure our cases provided a good basis for determining the merits of the improvements being investigated.

Linear programming is an optimization technique that was developed during World War II for military purposes, but lack of computing power limited its general usefulness. In the early 60s computers were coming into vogue. IBM had developed the 7094—a huge computer back then, but so expensive that most companies were reluctant to buy it to serve their needs. Seeing an opportunity, a firm called CEIR purchased two IBM 7094s, installing one in Arlington, Virginia and the other in San Francisco. Their concept was to rent out computer time to companies and the government, including the Pentagon. The Pentagon did not have its own computers, but Secretary of Defense Robert McNamara was seriously considering buying one. Availability of the IBM 7094 made everyday use of linear programming a reality.

Unbeknownst to us in facilities planning, Sohio's operations research group was developing a linear program simulating our refinery system. We got wind of these efforts and decided that this program could be of tremendous value to us. We began a joint effort with the operations research group, combining our knowledge of refineries with their knowledge of linear programming. The model they developed was humongous—way too big for practical purposes. Together, we condensed it into something more useable by eliminating unnecessary "noise" in the model, ending up with a very powerful tool.

Sohio's management soon became aware of the fruits of our labor and quickly realized our model could be used for purposes well beyond facilities planning, most importantly, optimizing daily operations for our refinery system. At that time, each refinery developed its own operating plan and was rewarded for the profits it produced—clearly not optimal on a system-wide basis. Management transferred five engineers, including me, to the Supply and Transportation Department, creating a group responsible for generating a monthly operating plan for each refinery. The refineries would be rewarded for controlling to their plan. Our group would also establish values for the various types of crude oil—light, heavy, sweet, sour—to be used by those responsible for buying, selling, and trading crude oil to secure this basic raw material for our refineries. And we would run cases for the facilities planning group to assist them in evaluating refinery capital expenditures proposals.

So good bye to engineering and hello to long nights running computer cases. CEIR charged $700 per hour to rent the IBM 7094 in the daytime, but only $600 per hour at night. (By the way, today, you can buy a hand-held Hewlett Packard calculator that has more memory and is faster than the old IBM 7094.)

With the advent of linear programming and its use to generate the cases used to evaluate refinery investments, Sohio's Corporate Planning group, responsible for reviewing all company capital expenditure requests requiring the approval of the president or a higher authority, was having difficulty conducting its review of the proposals coming from the Refinery Department. Those responsible for putting together such requests weren't able to explain to Corporate Planning exactly what changes would occur in how the refinery system would operate, thereby justifying the investment under review. Instead, they were relying solely on the differences in results produced by the linear program to calculate potential returns on the requested investment.

"Well, that's what the linear program said," wasn't particularly useful in conveying the understanding needed for a comprehensive review of the project in question. Paul Phillips, who headed up Corporate Planning, decided he needed someone with both refining and linear programming experience to properly assess the Refinery Department's expenditure requests, and he interviewed me for the position. Paul was a tall, lanky native of Oklahoma. After serving as a bomber pilot in World War II, he enrolled in Oklahoma State University where he studied accounting. He graduated, passed the CPA exam and joined Sohio all in the same year, 1949, and had been with the company ever since. Paul was very personable, able to use his intelligence and warm demeanor to good advantage.

Paul concluded that I had the experience he was looking for and offered me the job. My work in Supply and Transportation was becoming relatively routine, and I was itching for a new challenge. I felt that this opportunity would be a good move for me, and though I didn't know Paul, I sensed that he would be someone I would enjoy working for. I readily accepted the offer. But Supply and Transportation, claiming I was indispensable, refused to let me go.

Refusing to allow someone to be transferred was against Sohio policy, so after some debate, the higher-ups reached a compromise: I would remain in supply and transportation for six months while the department trained my replacement, then I would move on to work with Paul Phillips.

7. NEVER DARKEN THEIR DOOR AGAIN

I t was clear from early on that revolving credit would play an essential role in our financial plans. We intended to finance most of the pipeline and Prudhoe Bay through selling long-term debt to the public, and, most likely, a private transaction primarily with insurance companies. The timing of such offerings would not always be of our choosing, and so we would need ready access to other sources of external funds. Sometimes credit markets were tight, and it would not be possible to raise large sums of money. Or even if we could, it might be too expensive. At other times, material, confidential things going on within Sohio could present a problem. Our negotiations with BP were a prime example of this. Until we were in a position to disclose what was taking place, we would be precluded from going to the public marketplace for funds.

Revolving lines of bank credit, or "revolvers," proved to be an ideal solution to this dilemma. We could always meet our immediate needs for external funds by drawing down on our revolving credit lines. Then when the time was ripe for an offering of long-term debt, we could pay down the revolver out of the proceeds from the offering and start the process all over again.

In 1968, Sohio had put in place a revolving credit agreement with a group of banks that provided for borrowings of up to $100 million. We felt we needed at least twice that amount, and in mid-1970, we decided to arrange for another $100 million revolver. However, this time around, I wanted to eliminate the longstanding practice of keeping a certain level of balances in our accounts at participating banks as partial compensation for their loans: compensating balances.

Our revolving credit agreements had always carried a requirement that we maintain minimum bank account balances of 10 percent of the total amount of the revolver, to be increased to 20 percent of any amount borrowed. In other words, the minute we signed up for a $100 million revolver, we had to keep a minimum balance of $10 million in our accounts with the participating banks. As we borrowed against the line, we had to increase the level of our compensating balances by 10 percent of that amount. We always had a certain amount of cash tied up in our bank accounts, but not nearly enough to satisfy the compensating balance requirements of large revolving lines of credit. That meant we would have to borrow funds to meet the requirements. If we borrowed, say, the full $100 million, we would need to leave $20 million, or 20 percent of the line, with the banks, giving us only $80 million to use to pay our bills.

Although I didn't know when or why using account balances as partial compensation to banks was accepted as *de rigueur*, as opposed to other alternatives, I did know that it created some potential problems for us. I was routinely reminded of this every time I updated our financial plans and projections, which I did quite frequently. The process was relatively straightforward. Lay out the cash our operations would generate over the period of time under study. Subtract the monies needed to meet expenses during that timeframe—dividends, capital expenditures, etc. The shortfall—and we always had a severe case of the shorts during the time we were paying for our Alaskan venture—would have to be met from external sources.

In order to use our revolving line of credit to plug the hole, I would have to draw down 25 percent more than the indicated shortfall to have enough cash to meet the compensating balance requirements. In other words, if I needed $100, I would have to borrow $125—$25 just to cover the 20 percent compensating balances on $125, leaving the $100 I needed to be put to productive use. We planned to use a lot of revolving credit in the next few years, and the "unproductive" portion of the net proceeds from our bank loans would exacerbate the amount of debt we would incur. This would negatively impact our debt-to-equity ratio and our coverage of fixed charges—two of the primary metrics that would be used to measure our creditworthiness and that we already knew would be stretched to the limit.

To address this problem, the thought occurred to me that we could pay the banks a fee instead of using balances as part of their compensation. It should be easy enough to determine the fee they would need to offset the loss of earnings from the balances. Confident the banks would see the merit of my way of thinking, Paul Phillips and I set off for New York to talk with a few of the major banks participating in our previous credit agreement. We had two purposes in mind: get them to agree to participate in another $100 million revolving credit, and sell them on the notion of substituting fees for balances as part of their compensation.

Our first meeting with a lending officer at Irving Trust did not go well. He all but threw us out. He lectured us on how deposits were the lifeblood of the bank, and there was no way he would agree to an approach that would erode the financial footings of the institution for which he worked.

Our next meeting was with Citibank and it went better. The officers in their Petroleum Department listened patiently while I explained my rationale for doing away with compensating balances. Recognizing that our situation was unique, they indicated they would be willing to take the lead position in a new credit agreement and work on our behalf to sell our concept to the other banks in the lending syndicate.

"To be perfectly clear," they stressed, "understand that our willingness to substitute fees for compensating balances is based upon Sohio's special set of circumstances. It's a one-time deal. Don't even think about asking us to do it again."

With that, Citibank put together a group of banks willing to participate in a $100 million revolving credit agreement on terms that we wanted.

The passage of time proved that the bankers' "grave concerns" about adopting fees in lieu of balances were overblown, and it wasn't the death knell for the banking system that some had predicted. Within a few months, banks visiting us to discuss our credit needs were quick to note that they had come up with a new option for borrowers—either balances or fees were perfectly acceptable as part of their compensation for lines of credit.

As the old saying goes: "Success has many fathers."

8. BEWARE OF LIQUIDATING ASSETS

Compared to 1969, 1970 started off with a great deal of promise. Our deal with BP was effective as of the first of the year, and Sohio was now the proud part owner of five billion barrels of crude oil. The $150 million of proceeds from the first financing devoted to our Alaskan venture was in the bank, and some 3,000 miles away in Anchorage, pipeline engineering and plans to mobilize the construction force were proceeding apace.

The State of Alaska had granted permission to construct a small section of the supply, or haul road, from Livengood to the Yukon River, and that task had been completed in 1969. Although there were no permanent bridges spanning the Yukon, when winter set in, by placing logs on top of the ice and then pumping water from the river below onto the logs, an of ice layer some six to eight feet thick was formed. This "ice bridge" was strong enough to enable heavy equipment to cross, allowing the movement of massive amounts of road building machinery and supplies north of the Yukon. Construction crews would need this equipment in the spring when they, supposedly, would commence construction of the supply road from the Yukon to Prudhoe Bay.

This mobilization could prove to be an expensive gamble, however, since the permits to build the pipeline and that section of the road had yet to be issued. But the owners had updated and filed permit applications addressing concerns that environmental activists, as well as members of Congress, had raised, and the consensus view of the consortium was that the permits would be in hand in a matter of weeks.

Then there was the issue of Native claims. From the time of Seward's folly, Alaskan Natives had claimed they owned the land the government had purchased from Russia, but there weren't any contentious issues arising from those claims, so nobody paid any attention to them. With the discovery of oil on the North Slope and the potential wealth that it represented, it became clear that those claims could no longer be blithely ignored. The Natives, a broad term that encompasses the indigenous people of Alaska who migrated across the Bering Strait 12,000 years ago, saw this as an opportunity to press their case. The different tribes banded together to protest the building of the pipeline and started a series of collective legal actions at both the state and federal levels. In March, a group of Natives filed suit in federal district court seeking to prevent the government from granting permission to TAPS to build a pipeline across land they owned.

The prospect of an 800-mile pipeline running from Alaska's North Slope to the ice-free port of Valdez also served as a rallying cry for the environmental community. The institutional temperament of these advocacy groups ranged from moderate to extreme. Some wanted simply to ensure that the oil field development and pipeline construction would be done in a manner that was compatible with the environment, while others wanted to kill the project altogether.

A few weeks after the Natives filed their suit, the Wilderness Society, the Friends of the Earth, and the Environmental Defense Fund also filed suit in Washington's federal district court claiming that the width of the right of way TAPS was requesting exceeded the fifty feet allowed under the Mineral Leasing Act of 1920. Shortly thereafter, they added the complaint that the Interior Department had not complied with the National Environmental Policy Act (NEPA), which had become law at the first of the year.

The key provision of this newly adopted legislation was a procedural requirement that federal government agencies prepare an environmental impact statement setting forth the environmental effects of their actions before taking them. This meant that the Interior Department would need to assess all of the environmental effects of constructing TAPS before it issued any permits. Because no agency had every written an environmental impact statement before, no one knew what that might entail or how long it would take. On April 1, the federal district court issued an injunction preventing the pipeline from crossing land claimed by the Natives. A couple of weeks later, the district court issued a second injunction barring construction of the supply road.

The project was dead. Two injunctions plus a lawsuit, and the reality that no one—not the pipeline owners, not the Department of Interior, not the Environmental Protection Agency (EPA), or the State of Alaska—knew what was needed to comply with NEPA. And it was becoming more and more likely that, somehow, an accommodation with the Natives regarding their claims to the land would be necessary before the project could get underway.

Meanwhile, as attention shifted to the debates raging in Washington, DC, the Alaskan spring thaw was beginning, and the ice bridge was slowly melting, creating a real dilemma for the owners. Bring all of the equipment back across the Yukon, in which case it wouldn't be available until the following year, or leave it where it was? The decision was made to leave everything stranded north of the Yukon. As time passed, and with the end of the construction season approaching, TAPS decided to buy all of the equipment from the contractors because that would be less expensive than continuing to pay demurrage charges on the idled equipment. With winter coming, the equipment was mothballed.

Providing for the immense amount of contractor equipment would prove to be an on-going issue for TAPS. In March of 1974, a $185-million leveraged lease was put in place for the purpose of buying construction equipment because it was cheaper for TAPS to purchase the equipment and provide it to the contractors than let them buy it and charge it back as part of their costs. As an interesting footnote, when the project was finally completed, TAPS held a gigantic "garage sale" of used construction equipment, which had a significant negative impact on equipment manufacturers.

With construction in abeyance until the right-of-way permit was issued—more than 1,300 permits of one kind or another would eventually be needed, but the federal right-of-way permit was by far the most crucial one because construction couldn't begin without it—the owners of TAPS turned their attention to resolving the legal challenges and dealing with technical design matters. The ownership of TAPS had grown to eight from the initial three and was governed by a number of committees staffed by representatives from each company, an approach that proved to be increasingly cumbersome as a means of managing a project the size of TAPS, especially one faced with so many problems. To focus on the issues and streamline the organization, in August 1970, the eight owners formed Alyeska Pipeline Service Company to assume responsibility for designing and building TAPS. Alyeska was named after the Aleut word for mainland.

As the year progressed, debate over the design of the pipeline grew louder. There were a number of technical issues to be resolved, and certain elements of the design would become fodder for the environmentalists as well as the basis for the many stipulations that the right-of-way permit, when issued, would impose on Alyeska. Permafrost and river crossings played roles in how much of the pipeline could be buried (the conventional approach), versus how much had to be elevated, a mode of construction that would be hundreds of millions of dollars more expensive. Because the oil moving through the pipeline was hot, if buried in areas where permafrost was present, it would thaw the permafrost, a little like a hot knife through butter. Not a good situation. And in those instances where the pipeline was to be elevated above the permafrost, techniques to transfer heat away from the pilings had to be developed to keep the ground below frozen. Essentially, it was an Arctic "air conditioning" system.

With regard to the 34 major and 500 minor river crossings along the pipeline route, there were concerns that river bottom scouring caused by ice movements during spring thaw could damage the pipeline if it was buried, making it necessary to go over, rather than under, many of the rivers. Precautions to detect and survive earthquakes presented another design problem, as did a system to detect leaks. Properly addressing all of these concerns added significantly to the cost of building TAPS.

A new estimate of the cost of constructing TAPS was issued in November: $1.8 billion—double the original estimate of $900 million. To make matters worse, shortly after Alyeska was formed, the owners decided to change the ownership structure of TAPS from a stock company to an undivided joint interest. That change meant that Sohio would have to come up with the wherewithal on its own to pay for its share of the cost of constructing TAPS rather than ponying up 20 percent of that amount in the form of an equity contribution to the stock company.

Not a particularly good year, overall, for our Alaskan venture and the picture on the cover of Sohio's 1970 annual report conveyed a succinct message in that regard. Unlike the cover of the 1969 annual report, which showed a picture of a Prudhoe Bay drilling rig in the midst of winter, the 1970 report cover was a picture of a Sohio service station. A couple of paragraphs in Mr. Spahr's letter to shareholders was all that was needed to sum up events in Alaska.

> During 1970, excellent progress was made in the development of the Prudhoe Bay field, where our Company's leases cover gross recoverable crude oil reserves of about five billion barrels, supplemented by substantial reserves of natural gas.

And:

> Efforts to obtain the necessary approvals for construction of a trans-Alaska pipeline, linking Prudhoe Bay with the ice-free port of Valdez on the south coast of Alaska, are continuing.

Translation: about $70 million was spent on the development of Sohio's properties in the Prudhoe Bay field and about $53 million was spent on TAPS, but the pipeline was stopped dead in its tracks, and as of now, we have no way to get the oil to market.

Probably just as well they didn't let me write the shareholders letter back then.

9. Reverse Engineering IRR

The opportunity that Paul Phillips gave me to move from Supply and Transportation to Corporate Planning would open up new vistas, present new challenges, and would certainly be a good learning experience for me. I was looking forward to it. Although some of my training—linear programming and refinery operations, for example—would serve me well in my new position, to do the job effectively I would need to become an expert in evaluating capital expenditure proposals. I had conducted such evaluations when I was in the facilities planning group, but we relied on fill-in-the-blank forms developed by people who thoroughly understood economic evaluation. Unfortunately, they were long gone, and the people I worked for in facilities planning knew how to use the forms to arrive at an answer, but they didn't fully understand its underpinnings.

Fortunately, Corporate Planning had published an Economic Evaluation Manual to be used throughout the organization as the bible for determining the merits of capital expenditure proposals, and I decided I would use my six-month transfer delay to learn the ins and outs of economic evaluation.

Sohio used two indicators to determine the attractiveness of capital investments. The first was what we called the "Sohio Index," which was arrived at by dividing the present value of the project's cash flow by the present value of the project's capital cost, using the company's cost of capital to discount future cash flows. To index the answer, it would be multiplied by 100. An index over 100 would mean the project held out the promise it would provide a return greater than what it would cost the company to pay for it. The second indicator was the universally used internal rate of return (IRR), which represented the interest rate that would equate the present value of the project's cash flow to the present value of the project's capital cost. This rate of return could then be compared to returns that Sohio required projects to yield in order to gain approval.

In working my way through the manual, I had a good grasp of everything except the concept of present value, which was used to calculate both the Sohio Index and the IRR. I clearly understood that a dollar in hand today is worth more than a dollar in the future because of its earning power, but the rationale for bringing all of the cash flows for a given project back to the time of startup completely escaped me. I could do the math, and I got the right answers when I worked the sample problems in the manual, but I felt like I was back at mindlessly filling out forms without fully understanding the true meaning of the results I was getting. Given the responsibilities I was about to take on, I felt, somehow, I had to overcome this mental block.

Determined to comprehend this fundamental concept, on a sunny Sunday afternoon, I asked my wife, Karen, to take the kids somewhere out of the house to give me absolute peace and quiet. I planned to lock myself in a small room upstairs that doubled as a den and a playroom, and I was not coming out until my mission was accomplished. I started, once again, to study the manual, but the light bulb still didn't come on. Finally, out of frustration, I asked myself what it was that the Sohio Index and IRR should tell an analyst. My answer was that it should demonstrate the difference between investing in a project and not investing in it.

I reflected on that.

I decided there was a better way to establish this comparison than the way the manual taught. One that made considerably more sense to me.

I started with one of the sample problems for a $10 million investment. I envisioned that the company had two separate savings accounts, both containing $10 million. In the one representing the "do nothing" case, I simply deposited each year over the life of the project interest on the account balance at a rate equivalent to our cost of capital. In the other account, I immediately withdrew the $10 million and invested it in the project under study. Then, starting with nothing in that account, each year over the life of the project, I would deposit the cash generated by the investment and credit the account with interest on the balance.

Once done, all I needed to do was compare the amounts in the two accounts.

One way to do this would be to divide one number by the other—similar to the Sohio Index.

The other way would be to adjust the interest rate so the amounts in each account were the same, similar to the IRR.

As I got close to completing my calculations, using my new and vastly improved methodology, I began to fantasize about how satisfying it would be to explain to Sohio's experts how evaluations should be done. Finishing up, I compared my answers for the sample problem with those provided in the manual. Lo and behold, they were the same!

I suddenly realized I had just developed the IRR methodology several decades after somebody else had. At least I now understood exactly what I was doing and was on my way to becoming a world-class analyst ready to assume my new duties in Corporate Planning.

III

Years after I reinvented IRR, Alaska was preparing to impose a new tax on North Slope oil reserves. We retained Jack Lansdale, a partner with Squire, Sanders & Dempsey and an expert on utility rate cases to help us fight off the state's efforts. Jack and I were cooped up in a conference room at the Captain Cook hotel in Anchorage, waiting for the state's latest version of its tax bill. Killing time, we began talking about the impact of the tax on the pipeline's rate of return. Jack said something that led me to believe that, perhaps, he didn't fully comprehend the concept. As we got further into it, Jack fessed up that despite his longtime work on rate cases, his understanding of IRR was less than perfect.

"Jack, you're in luck," I said. "I can explain it to you in very simple terms. Suppose you have two savings accounts...."

It took less than ten minutes to educate him, and Jack was thrilled with his new-found insight.

10. GASOLINE ? NO—GAS

With TAPS hung up in the courts, there was no shortage of ideas—ranging from the sublime to the ridiculous—being bandied about for alternatives to a pipeline through Alaska to transport oil out of Prudhoe Bay. A pipeline across Canada to the upper US Midwest received a lot of support. The *Manhattan*, an oil tanker outfitted as an ice breaker, was used to test the possibility of getting to Prudhoe Bay via the Northwest Passage, the famed northern passage connecting the Atlantic and Pacific Oceans. Explorers and adventurers from the 15th century through the 20th had tried to conquer this passage with varying levels of starvation, scurvy, luck, and success.

The *Manhattan* enjoyed modest success in her trial voyage, but moving oil out of Prudhoe in this fashion was determined to be more expensive than TAPS. Because the Arctic Ocean is very shallow at Prudhoe Bay, some means of loading tankers moored miles offshore would have to be developed. A suggestion to use nuclear explosions to create a deep water port at Prudhoe to solve this problem was viewed as environmentally inferior to a pipeline. General Dynamics, a leader in shipbuilding and marine systems, threw out the idea of using a massive fleet of nuclear submarines to transport the oil. Both Boeing and Lockheed thought jumbo jets might do the trick. I can still remember a drawing of Boeing's proposed aircraft with the outline of a 747 superimposed on its wing to give perspective of how humongous it was. As a former operations planner, I had a hard time imagining having to factor in flight delays with all the other considerations. Blimps, rail cars, and trucks were viewed by some as alternatives that deserved consideration, but like the others, these ideas were fraught with practical problems. The one I liked best—I was unable to convince anybody else to take it seriously—was a rocket-like launcher that would fling individual barrels filled with oil to "catchers" located in the US. Imagine 1.2 million barrels sailing overhead, one by one, from the North Slope to the Lower 48 every day. Plus 1.2 million empties coming back.

Lots of creativity, but no good answers.

Without a means, pipeline or otherwise, to move Prudhoe Bay oil to market, our Alaskan project wasn't viable. Still, betting that attempts to get the requisite approvals to construct TAPS would ultimately succeed, the owners continued to move tons of equipment and supplies to the North Slope to develop the oil field. Developing Prudhoe Bay was a massive undertaking, separate from building TAPS, that required drilling production wells in extreme conditions; the installation of a gathering system, which included miles of pipeline within Prudhoe Bay; separation centers to separate the gas and water entrained in the oil; electrical generation facilities that would satisfy the needs of most major cities; permanent base camps to house construction and operating personnel; and a variety of other essentials. So given the fact that we were continuing to send a lot more cash up North than we were generating, my challenge was to raise money for what was, at least at that point in time, a non-viable project.

With all of the uncertainties inherent in our Alaskan venture, dipping into the public markets—or private, for that matter—for funds was out of the question. We knew that commercial banks felt the credit risk was too high, and understandably, wouldn't consider making loans for the project until the pipeline construction permits were granted. One means of financing development costs frequently used by extractive industries involved advance sales, production payments, or other similar types of transactions that were, when you cut through it, "loans," more than, as their name might imply, commercial transactions. Transactions of this type were non-recourse to the borrower since they were paid out of the proceeds from production, once development was completed. Because the obligation was a contingent one, it was not recorded on the balance sheet as debt. Commercial banks typically provided the funds for these types of transactions. However, because of the lack of construction permits, to rely on being repaid solely out of the proceeds of production from Prudhoe Bay was not a risk the banks were willing to run.

Enter Columbia Gas Transmission Corporation. They indicated that they had an interest in acquiring the rights to purchase Sohio's Alaskan natural gas—some 24 trillion cubic feet—if and when produced, at a price to be determined. The problem was establishing a value for that option. Seeing this opportunity as one of the few we might have to raise money, pending resolution of the challenges to TAPS, we began to ponder ways to use Columbia in a three-party transaction involving an advanced sale of crude oil in exchange for their right to purchase our Prudhoe Bay natural gas. Rather than having Columbia put up any cash, they would provide a guarantee to the banks, thereby removing any risk of repayment, while at the same time, under the most likely set of circumstances, minimizing the cost to Columbia for their purchase option.

Our idea worked. In August of 1971, we entered into an agreement with Columbia and the participating banks that provided for an advance sale by Sohio to the banks of $200 million of Prudhoe Bay crude oil. The banks got their security. Columbia got their option to purchase our gas. And we received the first installment of $60 million on the sale.

Columbia's option agreement existed into perpetuity, as far as I recall, so they likely still have the right to purchase Sohio's share of Prudhoe Bay natural gas. All they need is a way to get it to market. Good luck with that.

11. THE GLORY OF THIS HOUSE IS HOSPITALITY

Throughout the 1960s, oil companies struggled to find projects within their base businesses that held the promise of yielding reasonable returns on their investments. Consequently, the industry began to diversify, and Sohio was no exception. Someone came up with the idea of taking advantage of fallow land we owned along the interstate highway system. As that system was being built in the 1950s, Sohio purchased land along routes in Ohio for service station sites. It often proved necessary to acquire more land than we needed to accommodate a service station, leaving us with unproductive real estate. Getting into the motel business would put some of that land to use and would add another service to the motoring public to our portfolio.

Great idea.

All of us had stayed at a motel a time or two, so we were pretty knowledgeable about the business. Just to be safe, we decided to hire someone with hands-on experience. An executive search turned up Donald B. Campbell, the manager of the Peabody Hotel in Memphis. The Peabody was famous for its Peabody Duck March, a ritual in which every morning at eleven o'clock sharp five live ducks waddled from their penthouse suite, down the elevator, and across a red carpet into the marble fountain in the hotel's lobby.

Leaving the ducks back in Memphis, Don came on board and began the arduous task of putting together a plan for getting Sohio into the motel business, including spearheading the design effort, determining location criteria, and establishing a brand positioning within the industry. The result was first-class, and toward the end of the initial planning phase, Mr. Campbell came up with the tagline, "The Glory of this House is Hospitality." Hence the name for our new line of business: Hospitality Motor Inns (HMI).

Sohio's board of directors approved construction of our first motel at interstates 90 and 91 in Willoughby, Ohio, a Cleveland suburb. Shortly before the grand opening in the summer of 1964, Ohio began repairing the road in front of the motel, making it difficult—almost impossible—to get to it. Not an auspicious beginning for Hospitality, to say the least. For an extended period of time, occupancy and profitability were well below what was forecast when the project was approved. Despite this lackluster start, Sohio's board approved construction of a second motel outside Columbus on Interstate 75, which opened in May of the following year. This motor inn was an instant success, with high occupancy rates from the day the doors opened. Having thus validated the business model, Hospitality was well-positioned to proceed with implementation of its growth program.

Hospitality's location criteria placed a premium on nearby commercial activity and residential neighborhoods that would enhance revenues by utilizing the motel's meeting rooms, dining facilities, and recreation amenities. Don and the HMI team soon realized that only a few of the properties in Sohio's land bank met this criteria. Having to acquire new sites slowed the pace of bringing new motels on line, but in relatively short order, Hospitality was able to build up an inventory of prospective sites, enabling them to begin constructing new inns in a "cookie cutter" fashion.

Hospitality opened six motels in 1969 and 1970, reaching 11 inns in operation, with a backlog of attractive sites and aggressive plans for expanding. At the same time, we realized our Alaskan venture would take all of Sohio's financial resources: there would be no funds available for anything of a discretionary nature. Don and his team were stopped dead in their tracks.

As the one responsible for securing funds for Sohio's operations, Don approached me with a fervent plea to find a way to enable Hospitality to continue down its growth path.

One of the tools employed by Sohio was a requirement that those of us in management positions prepare annually a list of specific objectives that embodied the important things that we needed or wanted to accomplish, apart from our regular day-to-day responsibilities. In response to Don's request, I adopted a specific objective to find a way to finance the future growth of Hospitality Motor Inns without impinging on Sohio's debt capacity.

We studied numerous alternatives but concluded that the only way to meet this objective would be to sell 51 percent of Hospitality, leaving Sohio with 49 percent. At that level of ownership, Hospitality could raise its own debt without having it show up on Sohio's balance sheet. Since Hospitality would be starting off their new lease on life debt free, they would have ample debt capacity to finance future growth. We decided that the best way to execute on this plan was to sell Hospitality common stock to the public through an initial public offering (IPO). For good measure, we would throw in our Cardinal Systems subsidiary, which provided vending services to plants, offices, service stations, etc., since it would no longer fit with anything else we were doing.

Hospitality's results were integrated with Sohio's, so we had to break out a five-year history of its financial and operating results on a "standalone" basis. We also had to establish a capital structure for Hospitality, arbitrarily setting the number of shares of common stock Sohio would own, and, therefore, how much would be offered to the public. With the help of our Accounting Department, I put together an information package and called David Goodman, Morgan Stanley's partner on our account, to tell him what we were planning to do. I asked David if Morgan Stanley would be willing to lead an underwriting of Hospitality's IPO, and if so, what their view on valuation might be. David said he would discuss this with the firm and get back to me.

A few days later, David called to say Morgan Stanley would be willing to take the assignment, and that "the firm's view" on valuation was "in the neighborhood of $7 per share," or a little more than $5 million for half the company. I was flabbergasted. I had been using an estimate of $20 million, or $27 per share, for Sohio's proceeds from the offering in my financial planning for the corporation. Seven dollars per share was close to the book value of Hospitality's assets, and all of its properties were relatively new. The company would be debt-free, enabling them to leverage extensively off their equity base.

Conventional wisdom at that time was that the United States was entering a period of time when the work week was going to shrink, and anything that would benefit from an increase in leisure time was considered to have excellent prospects for growth. Motels fell into that category. Competitors Marriott and Holiday Inn were selling at 65 times earnings. I argued vehemently that Hospitality was a great growth story with lots of upside potential and any valuation should recognize this, but to no avail. I ended the call by telling David how disappointed I was, and at that price, we definitely were not interested in proceeding.

George Yaneff, manager of Paine Weber's office in Cleveland, had called on me from time to time looking for business. George's pitch: while Morgan Stanley was the "go-to" firm for bonds, they didn't understand the equity side of the investment banking business. But Paine Weber did. So I called George and told him I had an opportunity to discuss. We met. I told him what I was thinking and gave him the package of information. Excited, George headed off to Paine Weber's headquarters in New York to develop a proposal for our consideration. A week later he came back. His firm's view on price: $7 per share.

It made no sense to me to proceed at what I considered to be a ridiculously low valuation, so I shelved the whole idea.

Six months later, David Goodman called to report that the IPO market was hot, and investors were looking for merchandise. He asked if I was still interested in pursuing an initial public offering for Hospitality. I reminded David that our ideas on valuation were miles apart. Rather than argue about valuation, he suggested we prepare for an offering, circulate the preliminary prospectus and see what kind of reception we got in the marketplace.

"You're on!" I said.

I started drafting the preliminary prospectus, a lot of which was pretty straightforward. But I struggled with conveying the look, feel, and quality of Hospitality's motor inns in a way that would enable prospective investors to differentiate the company from, say, Motel 6. Then it hit me: a picture is worth a thousand words. We'll put a picture in the prospectus!

Once a decision was made to go to market with a security, our "finance team" would gather in Cleveland to prepare all the documents. In addition to myself, there was David Goodman, of course, who brought his experience and creativity to bear on each of our financings. Then there were representatives from counsel for the underwriters, Jesse Robert Lovejoy and Samuel F. Pryor of the Wall Street law firm of Davis Polk & Wardwell. Bob was the younger of the two, highly capable and clearly fond of structuring deals. Sam, the elder statesman of the team, had a quiet but forceful demeanor that provided adult supervision for the group. Rounding out the legal contingent were George J. Dunn, Sohio's general counsel, a close confidant of mine who was an extremely able lawyer, as well as H. James Sheedy from Squire, Sanders & Dempsey, Sohio's outside counsel, who participated in the drafting sessions, on occasion.

Notably absent from our finance team meetings was Paul Phillips. When we were preparing for our initial Alaskan venture offering in January 1970, Paul joined the team on the first day to get a feel for the process. Afterward, he told me that hunching his six foot six frame over a conference table for eight-to-ten hours put a strain on his back, and, furthermore, he had no interest in poring over the minutia of the documents. He was content to leave that to me.

As the team settled in to work on the Hospitality documents, I put forth my latest and greatest idea: include a picture of one of Hospitality's motels in the prospectus. My idea was immediately rebuffed with a chorus of derisive hoots. Prospectuses are dry, staid documents written in mind-numbing legalese to conform to strict rules laid down by the Securities and Exchange Commission (SEC). The team made it clear that the SEC would never allow the gravitas of a prospectus to be diminished by something as tasteless and out of place as a picture. My idea was totally unacceptable.

Sam Pryor was a great guy and a great lawyer, bringing to bear his wisdom and years of experience to find solutions to his clients' problems. After the boos subsided, Sam asked why I wanted to include a photo in the prospectus. I explained my reasoning. He thought it made sense and suggested we approach the SEC on a "no names" basis and see what it had to say about the idea. The question was put to the SEC, and within a few days, word came back that we could put a picture in the prospectus, as long as we agreed not to touch it up. It would be the first time a picture appeared in a prospectus. An unprecedented innovation, and just one of a number of firsts that we would come up with in our decade-long endeavor to finance our Alaskan project.

When one of Morgan Stanley's underwritings was filed with the SEC, a copy of the filing would land on each partner's desk. Imagine their horror when they opened up the Hospitality Motor Inn prospectus and found a colored picture in the centerfold! Morgan Stanley would be subjected to ridicule, and its longstanding and well-deserved reputation as a stodgy, white-shoe underwriter of the bluest of blue chip securities would be ruined. David Goodman's phone rang off the hook as one partner after another called to register his concerns. Having suffered similar abuse when I first broached the subject, I could empathize with David. But I must admit, I got a kick out of his predicament.

We submitted the first registration statement containing the preliminary prospectus on March 22, 1972. Two amendments addressing SEC comments for clarification were filed. Then on April 25, we sent a routine request to the SEC asking for an order to make the Hospitality registration statement effective as early as possible on Tuesday, May 2, 1972, at which time selling could commence. The night before the proposed effective date, after we set a price for the offering, we were at the printers preparing the final documents to be filed with the SEC in the morning. That, too, was routine. But there was a problem. The SEC examiner wasn't completely satisfied, but he wouldn't tell us what was bothering him. David was concerned. He had locked horns with this examiner in the past, and it had not ended well. So David arranged to meet with the examiner first thing in the morning to try to resolve the trouble. Hugh Mullen from Ernst & Ernst and I would tag along. Absent a resolution, the deal couldn't go forward.

Late that night—actually, the wee hours of the morning—after the documents were ready and everybody else had headed for home, I tried to figure out what could be concerning the examiner. Better to be prepared than be hit with a surprise at the meeting. The printer stocked a bar for its customers. I helped myself to a drink, sat down, and started working my way through the prospectus, looking for what could be challenged as opposed to what was readily defensible. I finally found what occurred to me could be the problem.

We had created five years of historical financial statements for Hospitality as if it had stood alone from Sohio. Our work was reasonably straightforward, and Ernst & Ernst had blessed the results. But there was one assumption that could be questioned. Hospitality's capital structure would consist entirely of equity, and I assumed for purposes of determining earnings per share (EPS), that all of its shares would be outstanding during the entire five-year period. Another way of handling this would have been to assume we would issue only enough shares each year to satisfy the company's capital needs. Using this latter approach, the number of shares outstanding in the first year would have been considerably smaller—and therefore EPS considerably higher—and would not reach the level of shares to be outstanding after the offering until the fifth year.

Why might the examiner be concerned with our approach? Perhaps he thought we should take the more conservative approach, which was to assume more shares were issued each year. During the five-year historical period,

Hospitality's earnings increased each year as new inns came on line. By using a constant number of shares, the growth in EPS would appear greater than would be the case if the improvement in earnings and the capital required to produce it, i.e., more stock outstanding, were aligned in each of the five years. Since our investment thesis was that Hospitality was a growth story, using an arbitrary approach that yielded a greater historical growth in EPS could be challenged as being misleading to prospective investors.

Here's the rub. For reasons that could easily be overlooked, that wasn't the case in this situation. I had considered both approaches when developing Hospitality's historical financial information. Because Hospitality's earnings were negative in the first year, had I assumed an incremental build-up of shares over the years in question, the first year's pro forma EPS would indeed be larger numerically, but negative, and hence, the growth in EPS would actually appear greater to prospective investors than what we presented.

Confident that I had found the answer to what was troubling the SEC examiner, I sketched a graph of EPS over the five-year period showing both approaches, demonstrating the approach we chose was more conservative. That done, I packed my briefcase and went home to catch a couple hours of sleep before heading to the airport.

At a pre-meeting breakfast to discuss our strategy, I showed David and Hugh my graph, which had a stain in the lower corner where my drink had set the night before. I explained what I thought might be the examiner's issue, but both men were skeptical. When we met with the examiner, there was a lot of beating around the bush, which got us nowhere. Finally, I pulled the graph out of my briefcase, showed it to the examiner and explained why I thought the way that we had presented the EPS data was preferable to the alternative. He looked at it briefly, said EPS growth had nothing to do with it and then volunteered that his concern was Hospitality might not have enough working capital. Would Sohio provide assurance that the working capital would be sufficient? I assured him that this was the case and that we would put it in writing. He raised a few minor issues that we addressed to his satisfaction, and the meeting ended. As we took our leave, I reached across his desk to retrieve my graph. To my surprise, since he had dismissed it as irrelevant, the examiner said he wanted to keep it for his files. I'll never know for sure whether my graph had anything to do with getting the offering back on track, but I like to think that it did.

That afternoon—at 1:30 p.m., to be exact—the SEC issued its order that our registration was effective, and the selling began. The offering was a success. At $34 per share, Sohio received more than $23 million. We got back everything we had invested in Hospitality while retaining a 49 percent interest in the company. Freed from the constraints of being a wholly-owned subsidiary of Sohio, Hospitality's future looked exceptionally bright.

Little did we know.

D. B. CAMPBELL
MIDLAND BUILDING
CLEVELAND

May 2, 1972

John Miller
1717 Midland Building

Dear John:

It is most difficult to express one's feeling at a
time such as this for words at best are inadequate. May 2, 1972
will be a memorable date for many years to come; the
ending of several years of close association with Sohio
and the beginning of a new and challenging future for
Hospitality.

There have been many people help write the success story
of Hospitality through the years, but no one who has helped
write the future of Hospitality more than you. Your faith,
perseverance, intelligence, warmth, sincerity, steadfast
integrity, soundness and all the other attributes too many to
list - have made our association such that it will be difficult
to adjust to the loss of your counsel.

We would look back over the rough road to getting here,
but now it would be difficult to recall the set backs and
frustrations - for the objective has been achieved and all
else is of little consequence now.

To you - I offer my friendship, my trust and respect -
for these are what I treasure the most.

Sincerely,

Don

GEORGE M. YANEFF
1021 EUCLID AVENUE
CLEVELAND, OHIO 44115

FD MAY 4 '72 J.R.M.

May 3, 1972

Mr. John Miller
The Standard Oil Company (Ohio)
17th Floor - Midland Building
Cleveland, Ohio 44115

Dear John:

    Congratulations on a very successful offering - the
market has proven your faith in the multiple you thought
the stock should command. My thanks for the generous
allocation both to me personally and for the special
bracket assigned to Paine, Webber.

    I hope I can continue to be of service from time to
time.

                              Best personal regards,

                              George M. Yaneff

GMY:ar

P.S. PWJ&C has commenced making a market in Hospitality
Motor Inns.

12. Boss, Mentor and Friend

Paul Phillips was a great boss. I first met him in mid-1965 when he recruited me into the Corporate Planning Department. At that time, Paul was serving as vice president of the department, and I reported directly to him. My title was economic evaluation specialist, and my primary responsibility was to review all capital expenditure proposals that had to go to the president or a higher authority for approval. An episode that occurred while carrying out my review function illustrates the kind of boss Paul was.

The purpose of the review function was to assist the business units in properly analyzing and communicating investment proposals so that the approving authority could debate the merits of the investment, as opposed to taking side excursions related to issues that were not adequately considered or communicated. When first put into place as a necessary step in the approval process, the heads of the business units viewed the review process as just another obstacle to getting what they wanted. Over time, most of the business heads, but not all, came to view the review process as a resource.

The product of our review was a letter to the approving authority. Our objective was to produce an innocuous, plain-vanilla letter stating that the analysis was properly structured, the alternatives had been considered, the critical assumptions and the rationales for them were set forth in the presentation, and the documentation was sufficient to enable a post completion review. If the proposal was deficient in any way, ideally the business unit would revise its submission. If we were unable to persuade them to do so, we would cover the matter in our letter, which would cause the approving authority to focus intently on it.

On one occasion, I was reviewing a proposal to expand one of our plastic fabrication plants that was running at capacity. I was struck by the robust returns indicated on the proposed investment because the business itself earned a very low return on its assets. The expansion would employ the same business model as the existing plant, so it was obvious something was amiss. The plant produced some proprietary products, but a lot of its capacity was used to fabricate products for other companies.

Digging in, I learned that most of the contracts to manufacture products for others were won through a bidding process, and the sales force was authorized to bid as low as necessary to win the business as long as they covered the out-of-pocket cost of making the product. The problem was, low-margin business wouldn't support adding new capacity, and the right thing to do was to eliminate it before proceeding with an expansion.

So the question became how much of that plant's current business, if any, was low-margin? I asked the analyst for this information, and after conferring with the vice president running the business, he told me that I didn't need that information and I wasn't going to get it.

"Fine," I said, "but understand, I'll have to raise the issue in my letter."

Next thing I knew, Mr. Vice President was in my office and he was not happy. He made it abundantly clear that if I sent a letter expressing my concerns, my days with Sohio were over. His exact words were, "Send that letter, and I'll hang you by the yardarm." He then stormed off to Paul's office. He and Paul had a good relationship, and I presumed he felt he could convince Paul to tell me to back off.

After some discussion, Paul (who later informed me of the conversation) told him, "Don't worry, John is not going to send that letter. I am." The lesson I learned: if you worked for Paul and you were right, he would back you to the hilt.

Soon enough, Paul came to have faith in my abilities, and since my review function wasn't a full-time job, he got me involved in planning activities, as well as evaluating merger and acquisition opportunities, which I found to be considerably more interesting. That ultimately led to what turned out to be an opportunity of a lifetime—responsibility for financing Sohio's share of the cost of developing the Prudhoe Bay oil field and constructing the Trans Alaska Pipeline. None of this was happenstance, rather the result of Paul's belief in me and his planning for my career development.

On the first day that I worked for Paul, he told me that he didn't do performance reviews but he'd let me know if he didn't like what I was doing. I ended up working for Paul for a little over twelve years in a variety of capacities, and true to his word, he never said, "yea" or "nay" about my performance during all of that time. Yet, I always knew where I stood with him, and the promotions I received spoke louder than words. As those occurred, Paul gave me greater degrees of latitude to carry out my responsibilities. By the time I took over the finance function, he allowed me to operate with a great deal of autonomy. Obviously, I needed to keep him apprised, but I was able to function freely with little or no interference from him.

That's not to say that we didn't have our disagreements. We did. And sometimes they were fairly intense. But Paul would listen, and because I was more involved with the details then he was, I could usually get him to see things my way. Such was not always the case, but even when I failed to persuade him, he never said, "Don't do it." He just wanted to make sure that I understood his concerns and that I took them into account.

Paul was not only a great mentor to me, but we became good friends. One never knows, but I doubt that my career at Sohio would have been nearly as successful as it was absent his help and support, and for that, I'll be forever grateful.

13. WINNIE WAS RIGHT

One of the key assumptions we had to make in our long-range financial plans was when the approval to begin construction of TAPS would be granted because that would be the point when our expenditures would start to increase dramatically.

We had a lot of debates over that.

Those responsible for working the problem in Washington kept telling us it was a matter of weeks. Paul believed it would take something like people standing in line to buy gasoline to get the federal government to issue the permits. Being young and naïve, I wasn't nearly so cynical, arguing that the logic of our case would carry the day.

And the Value Line analyst who had projected that Sohio's Alaskan venture wouldn't produce benefits for at least five years was having the last laugh.

Sir Winston Churchill, someone whom I greatly admire, would have sided with Paul. He had been warning the British Parliament *ad nauseum* that Germany was on a war footing. Based on the knowledge he had acquired through his intelligence network, Churchill was convinced Hitler's air force was as strong as, and perhaps stronger, than the Royal Air Force. And at the rate Germany was arming itself, it would prove most difficult—if not impossible—for Britain to maintain any semblance of parity. In a speech Churchill delivered to the House of Commons on May 2, 1939, Sir Winnie suggests that crisis is a necessary antecedent for political action:

> When the situation was manageable, it was neglected, and now that it is thoroughly out of hand, we apply too late the remedies which then might have effected a cure. There is nothing new

in the story. It is as old as the Sibylline books. It falls into that long dismal catalogue of the fruitlessness of experience and the confirmed unteachability of mankind. Want of foresight, unwillingness to act when action would be simple and effective, lack of clear thinking, confusion of counsel until the emergency comes, until self-preservation strikes its jarring gong—these are the features which constitute the endless repetition of history.[3]

Our political struggles began in earnest in 1971. The battle was joined on two fronts: the Native claims and the right-of-way permits. Alaska and the oil companies were anxious to reach an accommodation with the Natives. Although the Natives had filed a number of lawsuits on both the state and federal levels, they believed their best chance for success was to seek a settlement through Congress. The House Committee on Interior and Insular Affairs agreed that a legislative rather than a judicial settlement was the only practical course to follow. During the summer and fall of 1971, the House and Senate Interior Committees hashed out an agreement that was, begrudgingly in some cases, acceptable to all interested parties.

On December 18, the Alaska Native Claims Settlement Act was signed into law by President Nixon. The legislation provided that Natives would receive up to 44 million acres of land and would be paid $962.5 million. Of this amount, $462.5 million was to be paid over an eleven-year period out of the federal treasury, and the remaining $500 million would come from oil revenue sharing in the form of a two percent royalty. Payments were to go to 12 Native-owned regional corporations plus a 13th corporation comprising Alaskan Natives who had left the state. That done and out of the way, the only remaining stumbling block to starting construction was the matter of the federal right-of-way permit.

The battle to obtain the necessary approvals to begin construction of TAPS was waged in both the courts and Congress. Early in 1971, following the dictates of NEPA, the Interior Department issued its first draft of an environmental impact

---

[3] William Manchester, *The Last Lion: Winston Spencer Churchill*, page 149, (Boston: Little, Brown and Company, 1998)

statement for the pipeline project for public comment, generating 12,000 pages of testimony. One issue raised was the lack of consideration for alternatives to TAPS, something the courts subsequently ruled was required by NEPA. Eventually, all of the arguments—pro and con—were incorporated into a final version of the environmental impact statement—some 3,500 pages long—which was published on March 20, 1972. Secretary of the Interior Rogers Morton allowed 45 days for comments. The environmental advocacy groups prepared a 1,300-page document opposing the statement and submitted it to Judge George Hart, the judge in the federal district court who had granted the injunctions. Unconvinced by the environmental groups' arguments, Judge Hart lifted the injunctions on August 15, 1972. The environmental groups appealed, and on October 6, 1972, the appeals court partially reversed Judge Hart's decision, stating that although the impact statement complied with NEPA, the proposed right-of-way exceeded the width allowed under the 1920 Mineral Leasing Act. Alyeska appealed the decision to the Supreme Court. In April of 1973, the Supreme Court declined to hear the case, leaving an act of Congress as the consortium's only hope.

Turning their attention to Congress, Alyeska and the owners of TAPS began to petition the legislative branch to either amend the Mineral Leasing Act or create a new one that would permit a wider right-of-way, arguing that narrower widths, appropriate when mules were used to build pipelines, weren't sufficient to accommodate modern equipment. Hearings in both the Senate and the House continued throughout the summer of 1973. A bloc of senators from the Northeast who favored a pipeline through Canada to give their constituents the benefit of ample crude oil supplies continued to oppose TAPS but concealed their real agenda behind expressions of concerns about the environment.

Charlie Spahr was scheduled to testify at one of the Senate hearings, and he asked me to appear with him. Being ignorant of how oil companies efficiently moved crude oil around the globe from production sites to refineries, opponents of the pipeline argued that producers of Prudhoe Bay oil intended to ship all of their oil to Japan. When asked about this, Mr. Spahr suggested that Congress could easily address this objection by barring the export of Alaskan oil. Little did he know that this restriction, if imposed, would add hundreds of millions of dollars to the capital cost of our Alaskan venture.

The Merchant Marine Act of 1920, Section 27 of which is known as the "Jones Act," requires that all goods and services transported by water between ports in the United States be carried in ships that are constructed in the US, owned by US citizens and manned by US crews: "Jones Act Ships." No Jones Act tankers existed because there was no movement of crude oil between US ports, and the use of Jones Act ships in international trade was uneconomic. The ban on exports was imposed, and it became necessary for Sohio to build six large tankers to move our crude oil out of Valdez.

On July 13, 1973, an amendment to proposed legislation authorizing construction of TAPS, the Mondale-Bayh Amendment calling for more study of the pipeline, was defeated. Alaskan Senator Mike Gravel (D-Alaska) introduced a second amendment, declaring that the pipeline project fulfilled all aspects of NEPA and modifying the Mineral Leasing Act to allow the wider right-of-way. The vote on his amendment ended in a tie: 49 to 49. In cases of a tie, the vice president gets a vote, so Spiro Agnew, right-hand man to President Nixon, supported the amendment. The House passed a similar amendment on August 2, 1973.

The Nixon administration was clearly supportive of the project. On September 10, the president released a message telling Congress that approval of TAPS was a priority of his for the remainder of the 1973 congressional session. While this was welcome news, the crisis that both Paul and Winnie had said would be necessary to get political action was looming on the horizon.

On October 17, 1973, the Organization of Arab Petroleum Exporting Countries announced an embargo against the United States in retaliation for its support of Israel during the Yom Kippur War. The price of crude oil, which had been around $3.50 per barrel, rose to more than $10 per barrel. Gasoline prices followed suit. Shortages developed, and soon people were waiting in line to buy gasoline. The public began demanding action. Congress, feeling the pressure, created the Trans-Alaska Pipeline Authorization Act, which removed all of the legal barriers to its construction. The House approved it by a large margin on November 2, and the next day, the Senate passed it by an 80 to 5 vote, with 15 senators abstaining.

President Nixon signed the bill on November 16, and on January 23, 1974, Secretary Morton and representatives of the participating companies signed the grant of right-of-way for the Trans Alaska Pipeline—four and a half years after it was applied for, and a little more than four years after we entered the fray. During this timeframe, Alyeska expended approximately 1,500 man-years in designing the pipeline, testing methods of construction under Arctic conditions, and developing engineering and construction procedures designed to protect the environment.

For our part, by the end of 1973, Sohio had invested over $400 million in our Alaskan venture, and pipeline construction had yet to begin. To put that in perspective, at the time of our transaction with BP, Sohio's total assets were a little less than $800 million.

14. FINANCIAL PRESSURES MOUNT

As 1973 was drawing to a close, commercial banks were convinced that approvals for the construction of TAPS would be forthcoming. Well aware that Sohio's needs for funds were going to increase dramatically, the banks, being in a mood to lend, began talking to us about putting some kind of credit agreement in place. We were interested for obvious reasons, and we focused on structuring a carved-out production payment. Under this arrangement, the banks would have claims on our Prudhoe Bay reserves, and their "loan" to Sohio would be repaid out of the proceeds from the sale of our North Slope crude oil production. Properly structured, and in accordance with GAAP, we would avoid recording the advance as debt on our balance sheet. Instead, the obligation would be booked as a liability labeled "deferred revenue."

There were a few wrinkles to iron out. The transaction had to be designed in a way that wouldn't create a conflict with the advance sale of crude oil we had entered into with Columbia Gas a few years earlier. To address this, we used a claim on reserves, as opposed to an advanced sale, as security. Since banks can't own reserves directly, we set up a nominally capitalized corporation between us and the banks, a common approach in production payment financings. The banks would loan money to that entity, which in turn, would advance a like amount to us. The banks would receive rights to the reserves held by the corporation established to facilitate the transaction as security.

Banks in the United States have legal lending limits—that is, they can lend only a certain amount to any one entity. Because in this case the banks would be lending to a separate corporation, not Sohio, the loan wouldn't reduce the amount they could otherwise lend to us, clearly an added benefit. Casting about for an entity to take ownership of the corporation to be formed, Charlie Spahr, who was a trustee of Baldwin-Wallace College, a small liberal arts college in Berea, Ohio, a suburb of Cleveland, suggested that we use the college for that purpose. By adding a modest markup on the interest rate charged by the banks, Baldwin-Wallace could make a small profit on the deal.

The college was amenable to participating, and we agreed that $300 million would be the amount of the credit, to be reduced by whatever was outstanding under Sohio's $100 million line of credit set up in 1968 by the same group of banks. Repayment out of proceeds from the sale of our Prudhoe Bay crude wouldn't start until Columbia Gas had been repaid. All that remained was to complete the documentation of the Baldwin Agreement.

The lawyers ran into a roadblock in the course of drafting the agreement, which required a good deal of care to perfect the bank's security without running afoul of regulations, and to make sure it was worded in a way that would enable us to get the favorable accounting and tax treatment we wanted. Prior to its deal with us, BP had purchased from ARCO all of its newly acquired Sinclair Oil Corporation marketing properties on the eastern seaboard of the United States, as well as two refineries—one in Marcus Hook, Pennsylvania and the other in Port Arthur, Texas. ARCO was forced to divest these properties to satisfy the Justice Department's challenge to its acquisition of Sinclair. BP gave ARCO a note for $400 million in exchange for the properties and pledged its Alaskan reserves—now ours—as collateral for the note. When we did our deal with BP, we assumed liability for BP's note to ARCO.

According to the lawyers, the terms of this note prevented us from putting a lien on our Prudhoe Bay reserves without getting permission from ARCO. How difficult it was going to be to get a waiver from ARCO was irrelevant because there was no way we were going to ask for one. The owners of the Prudhoe Bay field had been engaged in serious and contentious negotiations to establish the amount of oil and gas reserves that lay underneath their respective leaseholds. Small differences represented significant sums of money, and with so much at stake, reaching a settlement was very difficult. Consequently, we were not about to hand ARCO a bargaining chip that could be used in those negotiations by asking them to do us a favor.

Because of the advantages in the Baldwin Agreement, I tried to find a way around this dilemma. Charlie Karcher, a savvy colleague of mine with whom I had worked on a number of projects, was an expert in oil and gas accounting, so I met with him to do some brainstorming on this thorny issue. We didn't come up with anything worthwhile, but rather than throw in the towel, Charlie suggested we talk with Earl Newcomer, outside counsel for the Sohio Pipeline Company, our pipeline subsidiary, and a lawyer extraordinaire. In my experience, there are two kinds of lawyers: those who give you all sorts of reasons why you can't do something, and those who are adept at helping you figure out how to get done what you are trying to do in a legal and appropriate way. I didn't know Mr. Newcomer, but Charlie assured me he was one of the latter.

Charlie made an appointment with Mr. Newcomer, and we went up the street to see him. He was a longstanding partner of the McAfee, Newcomer, Grossman & Hazlett law firm, which was obvious when we were ushered into his capacious corner office. Although he had occupied that office for quite some time, he hadn't gotten around to having drapes installed. Papers were stacked in piles all over the office, and his ashtray was overflowing with cigarette butts, giving away his habit of chain-smoking. He was small in stature, and his feet didn't hit the floor when he sat in his chair.

I explained our problem to Mr. Newcomer. He listened, then leaned back in his chair, and for the longest time, just sat there, thinking.

Finally, he announced, "This is not a sale of reserves, it is an incorporeal hereditament."

He called his secretary in and began to dictate. Although I don't think he used more than three or four sentences, his memorandum on the matter, when it came out of the typewriter a little later, ran a few pages long. Charlie and I headed back to our offices with what we needed to put the Baldwin Agreement to bed, which we did in January 1974.

Although I had never heard of the term "incorporeal hereditament" before, as soon as Mr. Newcomer blurted it out, I knew exactly what it meant. It meant we could do the Baldwin deal without getting a waiver from ARCO, and that was all I needed to know.

Talk about running between the raindrops!

III

Granting of the right-of-way for TAPS brought the magnitude of the task to secure the financing for our Alaskan adventure to the forefront of Sohio's concerns. To provide oversight of this extremely important function, the company's board of directors decided to form a four-person committee of the board, the Financial Advisory Committee. This group would review the company's financial plans as well as any specific financing recommendations before they went to the board for approval.

I interpreted creation of this committee as a lack of confidence in my ability to get the job done. Although I was relatively young and had no formal training in finance, I thought what I had accomplished to date was solid evidence of my capabilities. But it was what it was, and I had no choice but to go along with it.

General Horace Shepard, chairman and chief executive officer of TRW Inc., was appointed chairman of the Financial Advisory Committee. He had been the youngest general in the US Air Force and was successfully transforming TRW, a multi-billion dollar industrial company, into a global player. The other three members were Robin Adam, managing director of BP, a financially oriented Scot; Bill De Lancey, president and chief executive officer of Republic Steel Corporation; and John Hangen, senior vice president of corporate affairs at NCR Corporation, which had started in the late 1880s as the world's first mechanical cash register company and was now transforming into a computer hardware and electronics company.

Shortly after the committee had been formed, I had a specific proposal for financing to recommend to the board. I called General Shepard to set up a meeting with his Financial Advisory Committee to review it. The review was non-eventful—the usual litany of questions—and the item was put on the agenda for approval at the next board meeting. My presentation at the board meeting was identical to the one I had made to the committee. During the presentation, as was normally the case, there were a couple of requests for clarification. Everybody saved most of their questions until the end. After I finished, I braced myself for the inquisition that usually took place.

One of the directors kicked things off with a question.

Before I could respond, General Shepard stepped in. He commanded a great deal of respect in the board room and in a quiet but dominant way he interjected: his committee had reviewed my proposal in great detail and I had addressed all of the committee's questions and concerns including the one just raised, quite satisfactorily.

And then he moved approval of my recommendation.

The motion passed, and I was excused.

Out the door, I reassessed my initial reaction to the formation of the committee. Rather than being an impediment, I sensed it was going to a big help in greasing the skids for me. I had a long, hard road in front of me, but now this kid had a gray-haired, savvy businessman running interference. I sensed this was what Charlie Spahr had in mind. I should have realized he knew what he was doing.

III

The Trans-Alaska Pipeline Authorization Act was proving to be very expensive, adding hundreds of millions to the cost of construction. It mandated the use of state-of-the-art technology to protect and preserve the environment, and that mandate was carried out by attaching to the right-of-way permit numerous stipulations governing the construction of the pipeline. Those stipulations covered matters such as antiquities and historical sites, fish and wildlife protection, earthquakes and fault displacements, glacier surges and pipeline corrosion, to name a few.

Many of the stipulations were rational, and, indeed, needed to protect Alaska's fragile ecosystem. Others made little or no sense and were a complete waste of Sohio's scarce resource—money. A few examples of the latter follow.

§2.5.4.1. Permittees shall construct and maintain the Pipeline, both buried and above ground sections, so as to assure free passage and movement of big game animals.

This stipulation addressed the concern by some environmental groups that caribou would be unable to cross the above-ground sections of the pipeline, preventing them from following their migratory patterns.

In the above-ground mode, which would be about half of the pipeline, a gravel pad two-to-three feet high was laid along the pipeline's path. The pipe was placed on horizontal cross beams suspended between pairs of vertical supports with the bottom of the line resting four-to-six feet above the top of the gravel pad. Assuring free passage for the caribou and other big game animals presented a real challenge.

A couple of solutions to enable animal passage were developed. At intervals deemed reasonable by the interior secretary's authorized officer, and for relatively short distances, the pipeline was either buried in the permafrost or elevated to a greater height to allow bigger animals to walk under it. Where we opted to bury the line, it was necessary to install a means of cooling the permafrost to keep it from melting. Where increased height was the preferred answer, the distance between the gravel pad and the bottom of the pipeline was increased by an amount that would not only allow animals to walk under it, but would provide enough clearance to make it visually obvious to them that the pipeline wasn't a barrier to passage.

Five hundred and seventy nine animal crossings were created, almost one every mile. How to inform the animals where the crossings were located was an issue that was never resolved. After the pipeline was constructed, when the caribou wanted to cross the pipeline, ignorant of all that had been done on their behalf, they simply lowered their heads and walked under it.

§3.2.2.3. Radiographic inspection of all main line girth welds, and pressure testing of the Pipeline shall be conducted by Permittees prior to placing the system in operation.

X-raying pipeline welds for quality control was standard procedure for the industry. But typically only 10 percent of the welds were X-rayed, rather than 100 percent, as mandated by this stipulation. Because it's an expensive operation, inspecting a statistically sound sample of welds was considered to be a reasonable and adequate approach to detecting defects or irregularities. Perhaps there was good justification for increasing the sample rate for TAPS, but one has to wonder if 100 percent provided greater quality control than, say, 50 percent. And not only was every X-ray required to be read by trained radiograph interpreters, as an additional check, one out of every four X-rays was to be examined by an interpreter-auditor from the Quality Assurance Department.

Add that up and you have bureaucratic overkill and cost escalation.

§1.10.1. Upon completion of the use of all, or a very substantial part, of the Right-of-Way, or other portion of the Pipeline System, Permittees shall promptly remove all improvements and equipment, except as otherwise approved in writing by the Authorized Officer, and shall restore the land to a condition that is satisfactory to the Authorized Officer or at the option of Permittees pay the cost of such removal and restoration. The satisfaction of the Authorized Officer shall be stated in writing. Where approved in writing by the Authorized Officer, buried pipe may be left in place, provided all oil and residue are removed from the pipe and the ends are suitably capped.

In other words, once TAPS was no longer in service, the pipeline and all of its appurtenances would need to be removed and the land returned to some semblance of its former state. This new and unusual requirement for a pipeline would be an extremely expensive proposition. Financing the construction of the pipeline was going to be a challenge indeed, but at least there was good reason to believe that the investment would yield a handsome return. Presumably the owners would make timely provisions to comply with this stipulation, but if not, raising significant sums of money at the end of the pipeline's useful life in order to disassemble it was difficult to imagine.

These stipulations and many more made fairly clear what was required to meet state and federal government requirements for how construction must be performed. In order to remove uncertainties regarding the labor force, Alyeska entered into a project labor agreement with the major international and local unions whose members would be employed to build the pipeline. The agreement governed all labor performed for Alyeska and its subcontractors, and it prohibited strikes, picketing, slowdowns, and other disruptive activity by the unions, and barred lockouts by Alyeska to ensure that construction would be unhindered by labor disputes. The workforce, at its maximum level, was expected to reach 16,000-to-18,000 individuals.

In May 1974, work on the system began! Four years later than expected, construction crews, made up of thousands of workers began moving materials on site and building construction camps to enable work on the pipeline, pump stations, and the terminal at Valdez to get underway in 1975. Crews completed the 365-mile construction highway from the Yukon River to Prudhoe Bay in November 1974, and site development work, erection of camp facilities, and initial construction of tankage at Valdez was completed by the end of the year.

Alyeska's construction schedule called for mechanical completion of the pipeline in October of 1976, followed immediately by testing of the system. The pipeline, five pump stations, and the Valdez terminal would commence operations at 600,000 barrels per day in mid-1977, increasing to 1.2 million barrels per day by November when all twelve pump stations would be operational.

15. Ask The Right Question

When I moved to Corporate Planning in 1965, my primary responsibility was reviewing capital expenditure proposals. Since that wasn't a full-time job, Paul kept giving me more responsibilities. I participated in developing the company's long-term strategic plans, and investigated merger and acquisition opportunities of interest to Sohio.

Our strategic planning exercise, which included an assessment of the future business environment that we would be operating in, led the company to conclude that domestic supplies of crude oil were diminishing, and by the early 1970s, the United States would become increasingly dependent on foreign supplies of crude oil from politically unstable regions of the world.

At that time, Sohio was producing only about twenty percent of the crude oil needed for our refinery system, purchasing the rest of our basic raw material from our competitors. The burning question became: in an environment where crude oil supplies were extremely tight, could Sohio survive?

The non-rhetorical answer was: probably not for long! We needed to become self-sufficient in crude oil, and during the latter half of the 60s, we tried a variety of approaches to achieve that objective.

We stepped up our exploration efforts, to no avail, because we didn't have the expertise to succeed in that regard.

We tried to buy proven reserves in the ground. But opportunities of that nature were limited, so at best, all we could do was maintain our low level of crude production relative to our refinery needs. There were three or four small, privately-held crude oil producers that we were interested in acquiring, and although they were clearly reluctant sellers, we courted them anyhow.

Occasionally, we would get our hopes up when one or more of them approached us to see what we might be willing to offer, but it soon became apparent that this was merely their way of periodically establishing a value for their companies rather than opening negotiations. Important as it was to pursue all possible means of increasing our crude oil production, this particular avenue proved to be fruitless and frustrating.

One major publicly traded company that we kept an eye on was Amerada Petroleum, a highly profitable North American production and exploration company with no debt and plenty of crude. Charlie Spahr had a good relationship with the Jacobsen brothers, who, in addition to running Amerada, had a significant ownership in the company. He fostered that relationship, thinking an opportunity to broach the topic of acquiring Amerada might someday arise.

Born in Kansas City, Kansas, Charlie Spahr became, in 1959, Sohio's president at a young age. He grew up on a small Missouri farm. His father worked for Standard Oil of Indiana's Sugar Creek refinery. Charlie had a friendly way about him, a quick smile, and was skilled with a rod and a rifle. More important, he was a man of integrity, strong willed, well regarded, revered by Sohio's employees, and an exceptional businessman.

In 1966, we found out that the British government, which owned 10 percent of Amerada, was going to sell its stock, valued at about $100 million. It occurred to me that if that block of stock ended up in the hands of another potential buyer, Sohio's chances of acquiring Amerada would be severely diminished. Convinced it was important that we attempt to acquire the block of stock, yet knowing $100 million was a big chunk of change for Sohio and that we would have to secure financing to make the purchase, I met with the Sohio's senior vice president of finance, Al Wolf, and asked him if it would be possible for us to pursue acquiring that stock. After thinking it over, Al told me that, no, it was not possible.

A couple of weeks later, we learned that the British government had sold its stock to Hess Oil, a company I had never heard of. Back then—prior to the advent of the Internet—financial information on companies was most readily obtained by referencing huge bound volumes published by Moody's Investors Service. Out of curiosity, I looked up Hess Oil in Moody's and found that it was a small company majority owned by Leon Hess.

Hess Oil's balance sheet was anemic, paltry even, compared to ours. By way of assets, all Hess owned was two oil terminals in the Northeast and a small refinery. Clearly, if Leon could pull this off, we certainly could have. Studying the details of the transaction to see how Leon did it, I learned that he had borrowed the $100 million, pledging the block of Amerada stock as collateral for the loan coupled with a corporate guarantee—simple and straightforward.

At Amerada, the Jacobsen brothers were unhappy about the change in ownership of their company, and for a long time, they refused to meet or even speak with Leon. They tried to escape his clutches by arranging a merger with Ashland Oil and then Phillips Petroleum, but in both cases, Leon's ten percent ownership in Amerada put him in a position to make it difficult if not impossible for anyone else to acquire the company, and both deals fell by the wayside.

Finally, in December of 1968, Leon reached an agreement with Amerada's management to merge the two companies. To insure, as best he could, that the Amerada shareholders would approve the merger, Leon made a tender offer for more Amerada stock, essentially doubling his holdings, using an unorthodox tactic to finance the purchase. After the merger was consummated, he planned to have the merged company repurchase the shares he acquired in the tender offer. In effect, he was buying Amerada stock with Amerada's money, a fact that was duly noted at a highly contentious meeting of Amerada's shareholders that was convened to vote on the merger. Nevertheless, Leon prevailed and his company was merged with Amerada to form Amerada Hess.

That was vintage Leon: a very smart business man and a consummate entrepreneur. The son of a Russian immigrant, Leon bought a truck and delivered oil during the Great Depression. Over the years, he did what it took, within the bounds of ethics and legality, to grow his business from that modest beginning to a large corporation engaged in refining, transportation, distribution, and retail marketing of petroleum products. He also acquired ownership of the New York Jets along the way. Today, his legacy, Hess Corporation, has a market capitalization of around $20 billion, a tribute to his success as a businessman.

Years later, after production from our leases on the North Slope began, Leon became a customer of ours, buying crude oil for his refinery system, and I had the pleasure of getting to know him. True to his reputation, he was razor sharp and tough. At our first meeting, I told him how much I had gleaned about the practical world of finance from following his Amerada exploits. But perhaps more important, I learned a valuable lesson from this experience, one that I've never forgotten: I had asked the wrong question of our CFO.

I asked him, "Can we do this?"

I should have asked him "How can we do this?"

Although we might not have liked the answers and may have decided not to proceed anyway, at least we would have been mulling over possible alternatives instead of never even getting into the game.

Because our transaction with BP ultimately proved to be a far superior alternative, it was probably fortuitous that we lost out on the opportunity to acquire the 10 percent share of Amerada the British government was selling. Although buying Amerada would have gone a long way toward achieving our objective of self-sufficiency in crude oil, the management distractions to acquire the remainder of Amerada's stock might have precluded us from acting on a transaction with British Petroleum when that opportunity presented itself. Or the Department of Justice might have objected to a transaction with BP, had we owned Amerada. Although not always obvious when adversity strikes, a lot of times things happen for the best, after all.

16. INDEPENDENT THINKERS

Although the federal right-of-way permit for TAPS had been granted in early 1974, there were still some issues with regard to the ownership structure that remained unsettled, and until resolved, we couldn't get started on permanent long-term financing of our share of the construction costs. However, we knew we were going to need a sizable revolving line of credit, and that was something we could begin to put in place.

Buoyed by our success in completing the Baldwin Agreement, we were fairly confident that the banks had gotten beyond their concerns about the viability of our Alaskan project, and equally important, they were in a mood for making loans, something we felt we could use to our advantage.

Commercial bankers make sheep look like independent thinkers. Oversimplifying, but not by much, they tend to move in lockstep through the economic cycle. When recessions start, their loan losses begin to mount, and they stop lending, regardless of the merits of the projects seeking funding. As the economy picks up, the banks slowly start lending again, and over time, they begin to chase loans, easing up on their credit standards to put their deposits to work. It's at this point in the cycle when borrowing is easy, and the terms and conditions imposed by the banks are very—nay, overly—lenient.

Lucky for me, leniency was the lending environment in early 1974.

Figuring out how big a line we needed was pretty much a guesstimate, but I arrived at $400 million. The traditional approach to getting the job done was to pick a lead bank and have it form a syndicate. For reasons that I can't begin to fathom, I decided we would do the syndication ourselves. Taking into account the legal lending limits of individual banks, I laid out a syndicate that in the aggregate would have lending capacity of the desired amount with some room to spare. The group of banks that had participated in our previous credit arrangements didn't have sufficient fire power to get us to $400 million, so it was necessary to bring in some additional, larger banks. My "paper" syndicate included the major banks in New York, a couple in Chicago, one on the West Coast that had indicated an interest in doing business with us and, of course, our five Cleveland banks.

Thinking it best to solicit their participation in that order, I started calling the New York banks to set up appointments. I scheduled meetings with the New York prospects such that I could cover everybody there in one week's time. I flew to New York on Sunday—Paul was on vacation in Hawaii, so I was on my own—ready to start my first meeting the following morning. By happenstance, my first appointment was with Manufacturers Hanover, a bank we had not done business with before. Knowing that Sohio's financial condition wouldn't support the amount of credit we were seeking, I had prepared a presentation on the economic merits of our Alaskan venture designed to overcome what surely would be healthy skepticism.

I was greeted by Nat Howe, a senior vice president of the bank. After a few minutes spent getting acquainted, I started my spiel.

"You probably don't know a whole lot about Sohio," I said, "but we're at the beginning stages of a very exciting project in Alaska, and we're looking to put together a line of credit as part of the financing effort." Hardly five minutes had passed since we first said "hello," and just as I was about to launch into my presentation on the economics of the project, Nat interrupted me.

"How much are you trying to raise?" he asked.

That took me by surprise, not expecting to get into that until after I had finished my presentation.

"$400 million," I replied.

"How much are you looking for us to come in for?" he pressed.

Again, I was a bit taken aback, but I told him I'd like for Manny Hanny to consider $75 million.

"Is anyone in for more than $75 million?" he asked.

I explained that we were just getting started, and I couldn't know for sure what the other banks were going to be willing to do, but—that said—I intended to ask Citibank to come in for $90 million.

"Why aren't we being asked to come in for $90 million?"

I'm slow, but not that slow and, nice guy that I am, I told Nat if it was important for his bank to have a position in the credit equal to the lead banks, I was prepared to make that accommodation.

With that, Nat said, subject to being satisfied with the terms and conditions, his bank was interested, and I could "pencil" Manny Hanny in for $90 million.

Meeting adjourned.

I left the bank without ever discussing the project. In fairness to Nat, he probably had done his homework and was already up to speed.

I had a couple more meetings that day, and they also went very well. Similar to my session with Nat, the other bankers didn't raise any questions about the economics of the project, being more interested instead in pushing for an increase in their participation in the credit. I headed back to my hotel and reworked the numbers. Later that night, I called Paul. He had been skeptical about our prospects and wanted me to report in after my first day of meetings.

"Paul," I said, "we have a problem."

"I knew it I, I just knew it," he said.

"Not to worry," I replied. "I can fix it. We're going to increase the credit to $600 million."

By the end of the week, I had concluded my round of meetings with the New York banks. They all went the same way, with the focus on level of participation rather than project merits. Again, in fairness, some of the banks had participated in previous credit agreements and were familiar with our situation. Some had banking relations with other owners of TAPS, and, through that, had a good working knowledge of the economics of our Alaskan venture. And some of the banks had petroleum departments that followed the industry closely.

Nevertheless, I was amazed at how easy it all went down. I left New York with a "soft" commitment from all of the banks that I visited and with a reconfirmation of my understanding from past experiences that the competitive spirit often overtakes the need for caution.

By the time I arrived in Chicago the following week, I was getting pretty good at playing the game. My first stop was at Continental Illinois where I asked them to consider a $25 million participation in the revolver. The question, which I was ready for, was, "Is Harris Trust—a rival Chicago bank—going to be invited to participate, and if so, for how much?"

"Thirty-five million dollars," I said.

"Well then, either we're in for $35 million or not at all."

"You drive a hard bargain, but so be it."

Across the street, the same conversation took place with the folks at Harris Trust, and I ended up with a $35 million commitment from that institution as well.

A brief jaunt from there to the West Coast was short, sweet, and successful. Back in Cleveland, I made quick visits to each of the five banks with which we did business to acquaint them with our proposal. All of them were comforted by the participation of the larger banks and agreed to participate at the levels we suggested. That brought the total amount of commitments to a nice round $600 million, 50 percent more than what I had started out to raise.

All that remained was to prepare the documentation. A relatively plain-vanilla credit agreement with no onerous terms or conditions was drafted and agreed to by all of the parties. On the first of April 1974, we signed it.

17. EATING PEANUTS

Oil prices quadrupled and credit markets began to tighten, which pushed the United States into a period of economic stagnation. Several banks warned us that they might not be able to honor the lines of credit they had made available to us on an informal basis. Other banks that were part of our formal revolving credit agreements also expressed concerns about the advent of a credit crunch. Some banks even suggested we consider establishing a commercial paper program as an alternative to using our bank credit.

Commercial paper is an unsecured promissory note with a fixed maturity of one to 270 days, basically a corporate IOU sold to the public directly or through a dealer. Unlike other forms of securities sold to the public, commercial paper does not have to be registered with the Securities and Exchange Commission if it matures within nine months. Issuers frequently sell a new tranche of commercial paper to repay what is coming due, which makes available a steady stream of funds, much like that of a revolving credit. Talking to issuers of commercial paper, we were told that it was a very convenient and economic way to meet short-term obligations, so I decided to look into it.

Morgan Stanley did not have a commercial paper operation. When we asked them who they would recommend as an agent, they advised us to use Lehman Brothers. A wise choice on their part. Lehman did not compete with Morgan Stanley in investment banking activities, as did some other prominent names in the commercial paper business, so they were not a threat to take our business away from Morgan

Stanley. I made an appointment to see Lewis Glucksman, who ran Lehman Brothers' commercial paper operation. Lou later became head of that firm after deposing co-CEO Pete Peterson in a notorious battle for control.

At our initial meeting in New York, I gave Lou some background on Sohio and our financial situation, explaining why I thought a commercial paper program would make sense for us. Lou asked me how big of a program we were considering. I told him something in the neighborhood of $50 million. He laughed.

"Issuing commercial paper is like eating peanuts," he said. "Once you start, you can't stop."

Little did we know.

We decided to sell commercial paper under two names. We sold paper under the name of our pipeline subsidiary, Sohio Pipe Line Company, to provide funds for TAPS construction between take downs of long-term debt offerings, or "bridge financing." We also sold paper under The Standard Oil Company name to finance current corporate transactions. To further broaden the market, we sold paper in two markets, New York and Chicago.

With the program under way, I routinely figured out how much paper we should issue and for how long, taking into account such variables as our immediate need for funds, our best guess at interest rates at the time we would issue new paper to "roll over" or repay the paper that was coming due, and of course, the timing of our next long-term debt offerings. I was mindful of our agent's warning not to expect to be able to roll over more than $50 million of paper on any given day.

As I ran through my numbers on my mechanical calculator one day (remember, no Excel spreadsheets back then), I was about to write down a dollar sign when it suddenly occurred to me that this exercise was quite similar to the planning I had done for our refinery system, only now, I was inventorying dollars rather than barrels of gasoline or furnace oil. Linear programming, which we used for operations planning, would do nicely in this application!

Excited by the possibility of optimizing our commercial paper operation—to say nothing of getting out of all of the number crunching—I submitted a request to our Operations Research Department to develop a linear program for that purpose. The procedure was that if I wanted operations research's help developing a computer program, I had to submit a request outlining what I wanted done and why it was worth doing. Operations research would then decide whether to dedicate manpower to my cause and if so, they would estimate how long it would take and what it would cost to get the job done. Then if I decided to proceed, I would sign on as a sponsor of the project, thereby justifying their existence.

I was told it would take six months to complete the job.

Government does not have a monopoly on bureaucracy. I knew a model could be constructed in a lot less time. I also knew of a bright young man, Bala Ganesan, who was knowledgeable in this area and who told me he was interested in working in finance. I met with Bala, explained what I wanted to do, and asked how long it would take to get a something up and running.

"Probably about two weeks," he said.

I hired him to run our commercial paper program, making him the third guy, in addition to Ron McGimpsey and me, in my budding finance empire. True to his word, Bala had his program up and running in short order. And a sophisticated model it was, taking into account myriad variables and constraints that needed to be considered to arrive at an optimal answer to the question of how much paper to sell and for how long.

Bala's model covered a number of discrete periods into the future with yield curves, needs for funds, market constraints, etc. It would tell you what to issue with one exception: when we were working on a debt offering, Bala would override the program, forcing it to issue commercial paper maturing on the date we would be getting the proceeds from the offering. For example, if we were going to sell $150 million of debentures for delivery on the 1st of October, Bala would stack up commercial paper that matured on that day, knowing full well that we would have $150 million coming in to liquidate the obligation.

The only thing that I knew full well was, to paraphrase, "stuff happens," and so I worried a lot. One day, I grew concerned about our practice of counting on an offering closing on schedule in order to pay for commercial paper maturing on the same day. If there was a closing delay, we would fail to meet our commercial paper repayment obligations in a timely manner. An event of that type would damage our name in the financial marketplace and could be difficult or impossible to reverse. Our situation was such that our investors had to be true believers, and anything that destroyed their faith in us could be fatal.

Knowing that worrying can give you ulcers, I passed my concerns on to Bala. Better him than me. I called him into my office and told him to develop a plan to take care of the commercial paper that was set to mature on the closing date of the financing we were currently working on in case we failed to close. His initial reaction was just shy of panic, and he wanted to know what had happened. I assured him the financing was on track to close as scheduled, but I had decided it was prudent for us to develop a contingency plan just in case. As it turned out, the financing came off as planned, and I sensed Bala was a bit irritated that he had invested his time for naught. Nonetheless, I insisted on having a contingency plan in place whenever we relied on a closing to meet payments for maturing commercial paper.

Under Bala's leadership, our commercial paper program was very effective. In the 1974 to 1977 timeframe, we issued a total of almost $14 billion of commercial paper. The maximum amount outstanding at any one time reached a peak of $780 million toward the end of 1975 as a result of our struggles throughout most of that year to get closure on a private placement financing.

Little did Lou know how prophetic he was.

And eating peanuts was certainly an apt analogy.

18. New York, New York

I had been working in Corporate Planning close to a year when Paul called me into his office.

"John, how would you like to go to New York," Paul asked. "There's an opportunity for you to work in Morgan Stanley's offices over the summer and get exposure to the world of finance."

Although Morgan Stanley was not our investment banker, per se, we were using the firm to advise us on merger and acquisition prospects. One of the partners who was assisting us mentioned to Paul that, on occasion, Morgan Stanley would bring someone in from a client firm for a brief period of time to give them some basic training in finance, a sort of internship, if you will. Paul jumped on that idea, telling the partner that he would like to send me to New York to work in their offices as an opportunity for further development, and he was now broaching the subject with me.

Coming out of the blue, I found this offer a bit strange since my responsibilities didn't call for an in-depth understanding of finance. But Paul was persistent, almost to the point of being adamant, that I take advantage of the opportunity. Although I was genuinely puzzled about why I was being asked to do this, my immediate instincts were that it would be a fascinating experience.

Morgan Stanley and Paul had agreed three months would be about the right length of time for me to spend in its offices. Consistent with Sohio's frugal ways, the company would allow me to fly home every other weekend. I had two young children at home, and I needed to make sure my wife, Karen, would be okay with it. I told Paul I needed to talk it over with her. She is a very capable woman, and assured me that if this was something I wanted to do, she could manage the household in my absence. I told Paul I would do it, final arrangements were made, and I was off to the Big Apple.

Arriving in the city on a Sunday afternoon, I had minor details to deal with before I launched my mini-career as an investment banker. I had room reservations at a seedy, inexpensive hotel in Midtown. After checking in, I set off to deal with my first challenge. Morgan Stanley's offices were located at 2 Wall Street in the Irving Trust Building, and I needed to figure out how to get there. Cabs were too expensive for a daily commute. Besides, the cab ride in from LaGuardia had been nerve racking and, just as I was leaving the hotel, I witnessed a wreck between two of them.

Cabs were clearly out of the question!

Buses were, too. I had no idea when and where they ran, and I presumed they would be slow.

But I did know that New York had a great subway system! I found an entrance a couple of blocks from the hotel, and checking the subway map, I learned that I could catch one at that station that would take me to Wall Street.

The next morning, I headed for the subway entrance, rode down the escalator, and when I got to the platform, it was empty because the train was just leaving.

No problem, I thought. *Another one will come along in a few minutes.*

By the time the next train arrived, what seemed like a thousand people had joined me on the platform. And when the next train pulled up, it was chock-full of people, faces pressed against the windows in the door. There clearly was no room for anybody else to board. The doors opened. Everybody on the platform boarded the train but me, and the subway departed.

I was, once again, alone on the platform but was soon joined by another thousand people, or so.

The next train that rolled into the station was also jam-packed. Recognizing this was going to be different than taking Cleveland's Rapid Transit, I elbowed my way past a couple of old ladies and got on.

It was summer; the station and the trains were hotter than hell. There were all types of people on the train, but I couldn't help but notice a "suit" who was apparently headed for Wall Street, too. He was nonchalant, standing up, holding onto a strap with one hand, and reading the *Wall Street Journal*, which he held in his other hand. Amazing: he had learned how to continuously refold the paper lengthwise the width of a column or two as he worked his way through it.

A one-armed origami expert. And despite the heat, he wasn't sweating—cool as a cucumber.

Reaching the Wall Street station, I disembarked, having successfully mastered my first challenge. I showed up early at 2 Wall Street where Morgan Stanley occupied three floors. No sooner had I arrived when a partner called me into his office and told me that they were just starting to work on a debt offering for another client in the oil business. Concerned that the client might get upset if they learned that someone from a competitor was working there, they had considered calling off the internship and sending me home. But thankfully, they thought better of it and he wanted to alert me to the situation and ask me to steer clear of the team working on the deal.

Other than that, he said that I was there to learn, and I was welcome to get involved with anything else that was going on. He ended the conversation by reminding me that almost everything in the shop was confidential. Rather than trying to keep confidential information contained within the team working on a project, the firm's philosophy was to have, essentially, a "wide open" shop, expecting employees to know enough to keep their mouths shut. Should one of them fail to do that, the individual wouldn't be able to use the excuse that it was inadvertent—he didn't know—and the firm could fire him without thinking twice about it. Unique, but effective.

I spent most of my first week doing piecemeal work on various projects and learning my way around. To me, Morgan Stanley was the premier investment banking firm, relatively small with partners numbering in the low twenties and, maybe, 200 employees total (today, it operates

1,300 offices in 42 countries, employing 60,000 people). Each partner had a private office, but he also had his own "to die for" roll-top desk out on the partners' platform—a very impressive sight, indeed. Six partners manned the trading room, with four assigned to fixed income securities and the other two covering equities. A ticker tape spit out the trades that were made on the exchange, and this information scrolled across overhead for all to see.

The firm was putting in a central computing system designed by Wang, with terminals at everybody's desk, but that wasn't up and running yet. This meant that calculations were done the old-fashioned way, using industrial-sized mechanical calculators located in the "machine room" on the ninth floor, where you went if you had serious number crunching to do. That's also where they housed volumes of reference books—bond tables, historical stock prices, and the like.

As my first weekend in the big city approached, one of the senior project leaders told me something had come up, and he needed a lot of information compiled by Monday morning. It was going to take a major effort, and he wanted to know if I would help. I told him I would be around all weekend and would be happy to pitch in. I asked him what time he planned to get to the office in the morning.

"I'm going to be away for the weekend, so you'll be on your own," he replied.

That's when I realized what he meant when he said "we" would be working all weekend. "That's fine," I said, "But how do I get in? The office will be locked on Saturday."

"I'll get you a key," he said.

How ironic. Within a week's time, I had gone from Morgan Stanley being nervous about me being on the premises to having my own key to the place. I worked all weekend, and "we" finished the project late Sunday night.

A couple of weeks later, one of the partners, Alex Tomlinson, inquired about my living arrangements. I told him where I was staying. He said he had a sister who lived in an apartment in a brownstone on East 57th Street near Third Avenue. She was having surgery and would be spending the

summer recuperating on Long Island. He thought her apartment would be an improvement over the hotel and said I
could stay there if I wanted to. I took him up on the offer,
and life outside the workplace became considerably more
comfortable.

So was the working environment. The culture was very
different from that at Sohio, and I thought some aspects of
it would serve Sohio well. For example, when engineering
projects I was working on at Sohio were being reviewed in a
series of meetings at increasing levels of management, I was
always invited to the first review, but not any of the others.
But Morgan Stanley's approach was different. One of my
early assignments was working on a public offering of debt
the firm was underwriting. Not having played a key role, I
presumed I wouldn't be invited to the pricing meeting. To
the contrary, when the team was leaving for the meeting,
they turned to me and said, "Let's go." Off I went.

At these pricing meetings, the attendees sat in a circle,
and those working on the deal reviewed the state of the market, how recent offerings had fared, etc. Then the partner
running the meeting went around the circle, asking for each
person's view on pricing. At this meeting, I sat there, observ-
ing, figuring they'd skip over me.

"John, what's your view?" the partner asked.

Stunned, I managed to mumble something—inane, I'm
sure. I knew perfectly well that my view wasn't of interest.
But this was their way of training personnel. If you worked
on a project, you went to the review meetings, heard how
the information was used, how judgments were formed and
the rationales behind them. You were expected to assimilate
all of this and articulate your position on the matter in question.

They were kind to me that day, moving on to the next
person after my response. Had I been a regular employee,
my guess is someone might have said, "How in the hell did
you come up with that?"

I attended a number of these partner review meetings during my three months in New York. In addition to increasing
my understanding of finance, I learned another valuable les-

son: the sanctity of "the firm's view." At a couple of these meetings, there were very different points of view, and the debate became pretty intense. But eventually, things got hashed out, and a considered conclusion for a recommendation to the client was reached. From that point forward, this was the firm's view. Up until then, I had thought that the firm's view came from on high and was irrefutable. Years later, knowing differently, when I didn't necessarily agree with the advice I was getting, I wasn't dissuaded by the fact that it was the firm's view.

Over time, I got more deeply involved in a variety of projects. I was willing to do whatever was asked of me and to put in whatever time it took to get the job done. Working long hours was fine because I was away from home with nothing better to do, and the more time I spent working, the more I learned about finance. Activities ranged from the mundane—proof reading documents at the printers—to doing heavy lifting on major projects. And what later turned out to be very important were the relationships that I was building with team Morgan Stanley. In this regard, two individuals stood out: Dick Fisher and David Goodman. A Morgan Stanley executive once said of Fisher, "In an industry characterized by fiery, forceful personalities, Dick moved mountains by the power of his intellect rather than the force of his will,"—which was true of him in so many ways. He would go on to become chairman of the firm. Goodman, a senior project manager on his way to making partner, would become Morgan Stanley's partner on Sohio's account when we were doing all of the financing for our Alaskan venture. My relationship with him would prove invaluable. Without his diligence, tenacity, and creativity we might not have prevailed.

Toward the end of my internship, I was given a key role in a sizeable project. Morgan Stanley was trying to win a large paper company as a client. A meeting had been set for a few of the partners to make a sales pitch. In addition to the usual investment bank rankings and a listing of all of the underwritings the firm had done, the presentation was to include a *pièce de résistance*: a detailed analysis of the paper industry that would illustrate Morgan Stanley's analytical capabilities. My assignment was to pull together the latter part of the presentation. After several weeks of research and number crunching, I compiled a comprehensive comparison of thirty four companies in the industry.

All I needed to do now was get Morgan Stanley's Graphics Department to do my work justice.

At Sohio, we had a great Graphics Department capable of producing first-class presentations, using drafting tables, compasses, triangles, T-squares, and the like (remember, this was before desk top publishing). Morgan Stanley's graphics capabilities were considerably more primitive than Sohio's. I was convinced that Wite-Out was a line item in that department's budget.

Finally, in the nick of time, the presentation was ready for a review by the partners who were going to use it. The review went well, but the partners made suggestions for two or three changes. But there was a hitch: the partners were about to head uptown for the meeting with the prospective client, making revisions out of the question.

Being a perfectionist, I wanted to give it a shot. I had a couple of quick calculations to make, and then the Graphics Department could revise the presentation in short order.

But the partners' car was waiting, and they needed to leave immediately in order to make the meeting on time. Having made the trip uptown by car a few times, I knew it would be slow going. So I suggested they take the original presentation—Plan B—and leave. I would get the revisions made, run to the subway station, grab a train uptown, and meet them at the client's office: Plan A.

When the partners' car pulled up, I was waiting for them at the entrance to the client's building.

Plan A worked! And Morgan Stanley won the client.

My internship was rapidly coming to an end. A wonderful and worthwhile experience. After about a week back home in Cleveland, I broke myself of the habit of constantly honking my horn, flipping other drivers the bird, and tripping old ladies in order to get a seat on the Rapid.

Back at work, Paul told me that Morgan Stanley had given me high marks for my performance. I attributed this to my prior training, my work ethic, and my innate desire to excel in all that I do. My engineering pragmatism probably helped as well.

Only years later did I learn that Morgan Stanley had wanted to offer me a job. Seeking Sohio's approval, they mentioned this to Charlie Spahr. He told them that if they did, they would never work for Sohio again.

So much for the road not taken.

Sohio's finance team, left to right: financial planning associate, Bob Shockey; vice president and general counsel, George Dunn; manager financial planning, Ron McGimpsey; attorney Karen Shanahan; the author; and senior vice president for finance and planning, Paul Phillips. Bala Ganesan is absent from the photo. Reprinted from Prudential Magazine.

Members of the Morgan Stanley team who worked on Sohio/BP Trans Alaska Pipeline Capital's $1.75 billion private placement. · Front row, left to right: managing directors Ray Gary, Dick Fisher and David Goodman. Back row, left to right: Michael Brooks; managing director Judson Reis; and Robert Jones. Reprinted from Prudential Magazine.

The Trans Alaska Pipeline crosses more than 500 rivers and streams, 34 of which were classified as major. In March of 1975, the first pipe was installed at the Tonsina River crossing, about 75 miles north of Valdez. Courtesy of Alyeska Pipeline Service Company.

The Trans Alaska Pipeline traverses some of the most rugged terrain in North America, crossing one major earthquake zone and three major mountain ranges, and reaching its highest elevation of 4,800 feet at Dietrich Pass in the Brooks Range. Construction in Keystone Canyon and Thompson Pass presented special problems: There are three separate slopes on the face of the pass. The top and middle slopes are very steep, reaching grades of forty seven degrees. Courtesy of Alyeska Pipeline Service Company.

Special thermal devices were installed on about 70 percent of the 78,000 vertical support members to ensure that the permafrost remains in stable condition. The "heat pipes," which contain a refrigerant, super cool the permafrost by transferring heat from the ground to the air through radiator fins–essentially, an Arctic "air conditioning" system. Courtesy of Alyeska Pipeline Service Company.

Large prefabricated modular facilities constructed in the lower 48 states were shipped by barge (some the size of a football field) to Prudhoe Bay for final assembly. For about three weeks of nearly every year, wind blows the ice away from the shore, and conditions permit barge movements around Point Barrow, Alaska to Prudhoe Bay. Prefabrication significantly reduced the time and cost to install these facilities in harsh Arctic conditions. Courtesy of Alyeska Pipeline Service Company.

EXHIBIT 1: SOHIO ALASKAN PROJECT FINANCINGS
(dollars in millions)

DATE	AMOUNT	RATE/MATURITY	COMMENTS
July 10, 1969	$100	7.6%-1999	Standard Oil Debentures. Proceeds to be used for obligations that needed funding prior to our amalgamation with BP.
January 29, 1970	$150	8½%-2000	Standard Oil Debentures.
October 1, 1970	$100	N/M	Revolving Credit.
August 3, 1971	$200	N/M	Advance sale of crude oil to Columbia Gas Transmission Corporation. Later reduced to $175 due to construction delays and lower estimates of gas reserves.
March 1, 1973	$100	N/M	Standard Oil Revolving Credit.
January 1, 1974	$300	N/M	Baldwin Agreement. Advanced sale of crude oil.
March 1, 1974	$185	N/M	Leveraged-lease arrangement by Sohio Pipe Line Company, along with other TAPS owners, for TAPS construction equipment.
April 1, 1974	$600	N/M	Sohio Pipe Line Revolving Credit for TAPS expenditures.
December 4, 1974	$250	9¾%-1999	Sohio/BP Trans Alaska Pipeline Finance, Inc. Debentures. $169.5 for Sohio Pipe Line Company's account.
January 29, 1975	$250	8⅝%-1983	Sohio/BP Trans Alaska Pipeline Finance, Inc. Debentures. $169.5 for Sohio Pipe Line Company's account.
September 25, 1975	$100	N/M	Revolving Credit Agreement with the Bank of Nova Scotia.
October 2, 1975	$136	N/M	Sale of two million shares of common stock of Standard Oil.

Date	Amount	Rate-Maturity	Description
November 13, 1975	$1,750	10⅝%-1993 and 1998	Sohio/BP Trans Alaska Capital, Inc. Notes. Largest private placement ever. $1,186.5 is for Sohio Pipe Line Company's account.
April 1, 1976	$200 $50 $75	7½%-1977 7.6%-1979 8%-1981	Notes issued by Standard Oil. The 18 month notes were of the shortest maturity ever publicly offered.
April 27, 1976	$250	8¾%-2001	Sohio Pipeline Company Debentures.
June 30, 1976	$100	N/M	Revolving Credit Agreement with the Bank of Nova Scotia increased from $100 to $200.
September 28, 1976	$500	9¾%-1993 and 1998	Sohio/BP Trans Alaska Capital, Inc. Notes. $339 for Sohio Pipe Line Company's account.
September 30, 1976	$500	N/M	Standard Oil Revolving Credit
December 2, 1976	$75 $75 $200	6⅛%-1979 6½%-1981 7½%-1986	Standard Oil Company Notes
March 15, 1977	$250	8⅜%-2007	Standard Oil Debentures
March 1977	$153	N/M	Financial arrangements for the equity portion of Sohio's six Jones Act tankers.
1977-Various Dates	$357	7⅞%-1987 8%-2011	Privately placed bonds for the debt portion of Sohio's six Jones Act tankers. Largest Title XI financing ever.
June 30, 1977	$350	6%-2007	Joint offering by Sohio Pipeline Company and BP Pipelines of Series A Marine Terminal Revenue Bonds. Largest Industrial Revenue Bond offering ever. $237 for Sohio Pipe Line Company's account.
August 24, 1977	$315	6.05%-2007	Joint offering by Sohio Pipeline Company and BP Pipelines of Series B Marine Terminal Revenue Bonds. $214 for Sohio Pipe Line Company's account.

EXHIBIT 2: SUMMARY OF SOHIO'S ALASKAN PROJECT COST ESTIMATES

Cost Estimate in Millions Of Dollars

Spot Oil Prices in Dollars Per Barrel

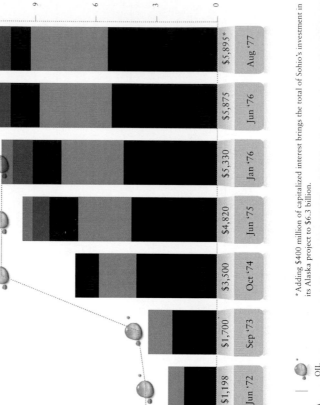

	Dec '68	Dec '69	Nov '70	Jul '71	Jun '72	Sep '73	Oct '74	Jun '75	Jan '76	Jun '76	Aug '77
	$500	$558	$695	$888	$1,198	$1,700	$3,500	$4,820	$5,330	$5,875	$5,895*

Legend:
- TAPS
- PRUDHOE BAY
- TANKERS
- PACTEX PIPELINE
- ALASKA TAX
- OIL PRICES

*Adding $400 million of capitalized interest brings the total of Sohio's investment in its Alaska project to $6.3 billion.

Because the crude oil moving through the pipeline is hot, the line has to be elevated above ice-rich permafrost. More than half of the 800-mile pipeline is elevated (a considerably more expensive mode of construction) rather than buried, the conventional construction mode. The above-ground pipe is insulated to further protect the permafrost, as well as to prevent the oil from thickening during emergency shutdowns or periods of decreased flow. Courtesy of Alyeska Pipeline Service Company.

On August 18, 1978, the author (left) joined California Gov. Jerry Brown (middle) and Southern California Edison executive vice president Howard Allen (right) in a press conference to announce Sohio's $78 million investment in emissions-reducing equipment at one of Edison's power plants. The investment was intended to offset pollution at Sohio's proposed Longbeach oil terminal, the western end of a 1,000 mile pipeline to transport Prudhoe Bay crude oil from California to Midland, Texas.

Conditions were harsh on the North Slope, wreaking havoc with productivity, and making construction extremely difficult and expensive. Aligning a section of pipe on one of the steepest sections of Thompson Pass proved to be a difficult task. Courtesy of Alyeska Pipeline Service Company.

The Trans-Alaska Pipeline Authorization Act aims to protect the state's fragile ecosystem, requiring 579 animal crossings to ensure free passage of big game animals. Twenty five crossings were created by burying the line in the permafrost, and 554 by elevating the pipeline to a greater height to allow the bigger animals to walk under it. In some instances in which the pipeline is buried, refrigerated brine is circulated through small pipes installed alongside to cool and protect the permafrost. Courtesy of Alyeska Pipeline Service Company.

19. WHOLE NEW APPROACH

Initially, TAPS was to be organized as a stock company, capitalized with 20 percent equity and 80 percent debt. Each owner was expected to contribute equity in proportion to its ownership and enter into a throughput agreement that would serve as a quasi-guarantee of their proportionate share of the debt to be raised by the pipeline. Even though Sohio owned 27.5 percent of TAPS, we would need to cough up only enough cash to cover 5.5 percent of the pipeline's cost (our 27.5 percent share of the 20 percent equity). However, at the time Alyeska was formed in 1970, the pipeline owners' decided, quite unexpectedly, that TAPS should be organized not as a stock company but as an undivided joint interest. Alyeska would be responsible for managing the construction of the pipeline and its day-to-day operation, upon completion, but it would not have ownership in the system.

Under the undivided joint interest form of ownership, each participant owns a share of the pipeline system as its exclusive property and is required to contribute its corresponding share of the total cost to build it. As a result of this change, Sohio would need to come up with 27.5 percent of the cost to construct TAPS—five times more than was the case under the stock company approach. Each TAPS owner would use its share of the system as an independent common carrier, separately publishing tariffs, that is, rates that producers would pay to ship oil through the owner's portion of the pipeline.

Shifting from a stock company to an undivided joint interest form of ownership centered on the fact that if TAPS were a stock company, only one tariff would be posted for the shipment of Prudhoe Bay oil. Under the undivided joint interest form of ownership, there would be as many tariffs as there were pipeline owners. That outcome, the thinking went, would be more palatable to Alaska, which owned one-eighth of the production from Prudhoe Bay in the form of a royalty. The royalty is calculated as the price of oil sold in the marketplace less the cost of transporting it there, so Alaska had a keen interest in keeping tariffs low to increase its royalty payments. From the state's perspective, competition among the numerous "pipelines" would keep the tariffs lower than would be the case with a single pipeline.

While there was merit in keeping Alaska happy, I always felt there were two other unspoken reasons for the change in ownership form. First, in the original stock company format, the cost of debt to be issued by the stock company would reflect the blended creditworthiness of the participants. Those owners with strong balance sheets, Exxon in particular, would be penalized financially by the participation of those of us who had weaker credit ratings; interest rates for debt would be higher to reflect the lower creditworthiness of the weaker participants. Second, attributing Machiavellian motivations to our partners, if Sohio found it impossible to raise enough money in the financial markets to meet its capital needs, we most likely would be forced to sell a portion of our reserves in Alaska. Oil being hard—and expensive—to find, there was no doubt that our competitors would love to get their hands on our reserves. Putting additional financial pressure on Sohio certainly wouldn't hurt and could possible help them.

Due primarily to the delays in receiving approvals to construct TAPS, Alyeska announced in 1974 that the initial capacity of the system would double from 600 thousand to 1.2 million barrels per day. That event, along with ever-increasing construction costs, precipitated discussion among the owners as to who was going to own how much of the larger system. Of paramount importance was the prevailing thinking that ownership of TAPS should correspond to ownership of oil in the Prudhoe Bay field. Sohio owned a little more than 53 percent of the oil reserves at Prudhoe Bay, but only 27.5 percent of TAPS. After some tough negotiations, in July of 1974, Alyeska announced that the ownership in TAPS had changed. Three of the five smaller players—Union Oil, Phillips Petroleum, and Amerada Hess kept the same capacity, barrel-wise, in the expanded pipeline by cutting their ownership in half. Mobil moved down to five percent. Home of Canada dropped out. ARCO, which owned a little more than 20 percent of the oil reserves in Prudhoe, reduced its interest in TAPS to 21 percent. Exxon, whose ownership in Prudhoe was the same as ARCO's, dropped its ownership in TAPS to 20 percent. Sohio, the odd man out, ended up begrudgingly agreeing to increase its ownership from 27.5 percent to a little over 49 percent.

This was a real double whammy for Sohio: a change in the ownership structure that required us to finance 100 percent of our share of the cost of constructing TAPS, rather than a 20 percent equity contribution, and an increase in ownership of the system to almost one-half.

There was growing awareness that the desired outcome of the original deal between Sohio and BP was being rendered moot by the interminable delays and the greatly increased financial burden to be shouldered by Sohio. Both companies agreed to modify the terms of the special stock issued to BP in order to preserve the original intent of the transaction. Of significance was the "trigger" date when BP's ultimate ownership of Sohio would be determined. Initially, that date was January 1, 1978, unless production from Prudhoe Bay for Sohio's account had already reached 600,000 barrels per day. To provide reasonable assurance that Sohio would achieve the economic benefits from the production of 600,000 barrels per day of oil, and conversely, that BP would obtain the 53 percent ownership interest in Sohio it had originally contemplated, that date was extended to January 1, 1984. Also, in light of the substantial increase in construction cost to be borne by Sohio, relative to the cost estimate when the deal with BP was struck, BP agreed to acquire a 15.84 percent interest in TAPS from Sohio, thereby reducing our ownership to 33.34 percent.

Meanwhile, ARCO had developed the outline of a concept for a three-way partnership involving Sohio and BP that would serve not only as a vehicle for financing our collective interest in TAPS, but would do so in a tax-efficient manner. Because we were interested in any approach that would make it easier for us to meet our financial obligations, we entered into discussions with ARCO to see if the idea could be perfected. The concept proved to be extremely complex and convoluted, putting the creativity of the lawyers, accountants, and tax experts to the test. In the midst of these discussions, ARCO introduced the notion that, because it was bringing more financial strength to the partnership than Sohio was, we would need to provide ARCO with some vigorish to make the partnership equitable for them. What they had in mind was some compromise on our part in the ongoing negotiations regarding ownership of the Prudhoe Bay field.

For purposes of development and operation, the Prudhoe Bay field had been divided into two areas of approximately equal size. While there were multiple owners, there were only two operators. BP was the operator of the western portion, and ARCO was the operator of the eastern portion. Field operations were expected to be conducted according to a unit agreement under which all production from the reservoir would be allocated on a basis to be agreed upon.

Easier said than done.

Although there's some science in determining how much oil underlies the leaseholds of individual participants, it is not a perfect science, and the appropriate allocation was subject to hot debate: a minute difference amounts to a lot of money—in the billions of dollars—making compromise Sisyphean. And no way could we justify, much less get approval for, agreeing to back off our position on how much oil to which Sohio was entitled just to make life easier for those of us in finance.

On what turned out to be the final morning of negotiations at Morgan Stanley's offices in New York, it became clear that ARCO's demands were far too onerous, and they were not prepared to budge, leaving us no choice but to end the discussions—a disappointing and bitter end to what started out as a promising alternative for us. The Sohio team retreated to a private dining room, and we took turns cursing the long hours we had devoted in a futile attempt to find a resolution satisfactory to all. Someone suggested that a drink would help nurse our wounds. Serving liquor for lunch in a Morgan Stanley dining room was strictly "verboten," but we knew this was not the case for dinner, and we were in no mood to observe protocol. David Goodman was dispatched to find out where the liquor was kept, and he soon reappeared with enough booze to drown our sorrows.

It was clear that we—and BP—were on our own, when it came to financing our respective ownership positions in TAPS. We began to worry about the confusion that might be created in the minds of potential investors and creditors, given the relationship between us, with both of us raising funds to build TAPS. We also were concerned about bumping into each other in the financial markets. Some coordination would be needed, but that coordination had its own set of issues. For example, let's say the credit markets looked attractive—whose turn would it be to issue debt? And, having both of us in the marketplace at the same time just wouldn't work.

To address these problems, we formed a finance company, Sohio/BP Trans Alaska Pipeline Finance Inc. ("Finance"), owned 68 percent by Sohio and 32 percent by BP. The purpose of this finance vehicle was to issue debt in an amount sufficient to cover both companies' costs for the construction of TAPS. The funds raised by Finance would be distributed in accordance with each company's ownership. Sohio's finance team would take the lead in securing the funds for Finance.

By now, a good deal of the operational and political uncertainty on this project had been dispelled, and we were able to cast an updated financial plan without having to allow for wide variations. We knew how much of the pipeline we were going to own and how that ownership would be structured.

The design parameters for the pipeline had been set. Construction of TAPS was progressing, and its completion date could be estimated with some accuracy. Although, as history had shown, Alyeska's cost estimates had to be viewed with some skepticism, they now had more knowledge and experience on which to base estimates.

In October of 1974, Alyeska released its updated cost estimate for the system. Taking into account prior construction cost experiences and the contracts that had been let, the estimate totaled $6 billion, excluding interest costs to be borne by the owners, up significantly from the previous estimate of $4.1 billion. There were a number of reasons for the cost escalation, but doubling the initial capacity to 1.2 million barrels per day and increasing the amount of the pipeline to be built above ground to 50 percent accounted for most of it.

Fortunately, during this span of time, crude oil price increases kept pace with the system's cost increases, climbing from a little more than $3 per barrel in 1968 to over $10 per barrel in 1974. As a result, the return on our investment in Alaska remained relatively stable and attractive, but while that was certainly essential to our financing efforts, it did nothing to assuage our growing concerns over the dollars we had to raise.

The groundwork had been laid. The time to execute on our financial plans had arrived.

20. NORTH TO THE FUTURE

Until you see Alaska for yourself, you really can't begin to grasp what it meant to build an eight hundred-mile pipeline across it. Alaska's state motto, North to the Future, seemed apropos, a paradoxically barren existence but promising future. To give potential investors an appreciation of what we were dealing with, as well as counter a lot of negative stories in the media about TAPS—its infeasibility because of the harsh conditions and its deleterious effects on the state, etc.—we started an initial series of four inspection trips for representatives from domestic and foreign banks, pension funds, and life insurance companies to acquaint them with our project. We continued to bring investors up north on a regular basis throughout the construction period for progress updates.

Our tours were extremely interesting and informative, giving current and potential lenders a chance to visualize firsthand the magnitude and complexity of the project, the largest-ever private industrial undertaking. As an engineering feat, Prudhoe Bay and the pipeline rivaled the Panama Canal. The logistics associated with moving men and material to build the pipeline exceeded that of the Berlin Airlift. Climatic conditions were extremely hostile, and the stipulations imposed to address ecological concerns were demanding. Conducting up-close inspection trips proved to be an effective way to convey to investors a sense of the enormity of our Alaskan venture, as well as our ability to cope successfully with the challenges it presented.

A typical tour would start on Monday, with the guests flying into Anchorage and taking a quick cab ride to the

Captain Cook Hotel where they would stay. Dinner that first night almost always included a number of dignitaries, business people, government officials, state and local politicians, and the like, to give our visitors a chance to soak up some of Alaska's culture. The next morning, we would board a charter plane and head off to Valdez to inspect the terminal. We attempted to go there first because weather conditions made flying into Valdez iffy. If we weren't able to get in, the plane would make a U-turn and head for the North Slope, leaving Valdez as our destination for the next day.

These trips were long and grueling affairs, made worse by the time change, jet lag, and the amount of ground covered. For those of us serving as guides, four trips in one month was utterly exhausting. But usually something would happen on every trip to break up the monotony and provide a bit of amusement.

During one tour, I greeted members arriving in Anchorage on a flight out of Seattle, making sure they got their luggage and herding them into cabs for the trip downtown. I usually rode in with the last contingent, but on this particular occasion, I suddenly discovered they all had departed, so I flagged down a cab for myself. After putting my bags in the trunk, the driver stood on the curb waiting for another passenger so he could charge the two of us full fare. I was anxious to get to the hotel, and what the driver was doing was against regulations. Complaints from me to get moving fell on deaf ears. Finally, another gentleman who was staying at the Westmark Hotel showed up, and we were off to downtown.

The cab driver dropped me off at the Captain Cook first. When I asked him what I owed him, he said six dollars—the full fare, not half. Although seemingly no big deal, matters of principle are important to me. Besides, I was aggravated by the delay. I told him that wasn't right, and if he insisted, I was going to report him. He laughed and said, "Go ahead." I made a mental note of his cab number.

I checked in, went up to my room, and unpacked. I had a few hours before the evening festivities would start and planned to use some of the time paying a courtesy call on one of the Alaskan banks with which we did business. In the meantime, I called the cab company and explained what had happened. They told me I was correct: the driver should have known better, and they assured me that they would talk to him about it. They asked for my name and where I was staying, and thanked me for bringing the matter to their attention.

As I was leaving to make my call on the bank, I noticed David Goodman and a couple of our cohorts who were along for the trip sitting in the hotel bar. I stopped in to say hello and to make sure everything was okay. I told them about my incident with the cab driver. They thought I was nuts for reporting him, warning me that he would probably seek revenge.

It had been a long day already, so after my visit with the bank, I decided to take a nap before dinner. I had just fallen asleep when there was a knock at the door.

"Who is it?" I asked.

"It's your cab driver," came the voice from the other side of the door.

I knew better. The guys in the bar, probably having had too much to drink, had decided to pull a practical joke on me.

I yelled back "Can't be. My cab driver had an accent. Come again with an accent."

The voice came back with a strange intonation, "This here's your cab driver."

Hah! That gave them away. I opened the door. Damned if it wasn't the cab driver. I slammed the door. Then it occurred to me that this guy must think I'm stark raving mad, and there is nothing more disconcerting than dealing with a maniac.

I opened the door and asked, "What do you want?"

"I came to give you your money back," he replied and handed me three bucks.

Emboldened, I said "How about the other guy?"

But then I realized I was pushing my luck and said, "Never mind. Thanks," and shut the door. I got out my account of expenses and changed the entry for cab fare from six dollars to three. Not the most important thing I did that week for the shareholders, but every little bit counts.

On another occasion, we were flying through Atigun Pass in the Brooks Range heading to the North Slope when the pilot announced that there was a storm up ahead, and we were going to have to turn around and land at the construction camp at Franklin Bluffs. Our contingency plan for this set of circumstances was to load everybody onto a bus and drive them up the haul road to the North Slope, which we did. Traveling the haul road on a bus is not a comfortable way to go, and by the time we got there, toured the Prudhoe Bay field, and returned to Franklin Bluffs, it was getting late and everybody was tired. After everybody got back on the plane for the return trip to Anchorage, I told the flight attendant to make sure they all got a drink before we took off. She showed me the manifest across which was printed in large red letters: "No liquor on this flight."

Earlier as we were pulling up to our plane, I had noticed there was one other aircraft parked a short distance from ours. I recognized it as one of the small jets used by Alyeska. I had been on that plane several times, and I knew that just inside the door was a small service area where, in addition to a coffee pot, there were three fairly large glass jars with pumps on top for dispensing gin, vodka and scotch. Alongside were small plastic cups in which to serve the drinks.

On our tours, we always took along the individual who handled press relations for Alyeska. While in flight, he would provide a bit of a travelogue and explain to the investors what they were going to see. Concerned about having a group of disgruntled and unruly investors on my hands, I suggested to him that we try to get into the Alyeska plane. He was fairly tall, and when we got to the plane, he reached up, grabbed the door handle and pulled. It was unlocked and down came the steps to the plane. I told him to go back and get a few guys to help us. I scrambled up the steps and began to fill plastic cups with booze. Soon, we had a small brigade ferrying the booze back to our plane, where the flight attendant was dispensing it to the others. I pretty well drained the containers, being careful to leave a little bit in each for whoever was traveling on the Alyeska plane. I got off, shut the door, and returned to my plane. I had no sooner gotten inside and closed the door when a van came roaring by, pulling up next to the Alyeska plane. Two pilots and two suits jumped out. Within minutes, their plane took off. I came within a hair's breadth of getting caught red-handed procuring booze for my charges. But, since Sohio was paying its fair share of Alyeska's expenses, I didn't consider my exploits to be out of line, but rather a way to keep our investors contented, which would indirectly inure to the benefit of all of the owners.

21. A Taste of Finance

The summer spent with Morgan Stanley had greatly expanded my understanding of the art of finance, and I was able to apply some of this newly acquired knowledge to my work in Corporate Planning, particularly my merger and acquisition activities. Helpful as it was, my job required only a rudimentary understanding of finance, so I was still somewhat puzzled as to why the company saw fit to send me off to Morgan Stanley for three months. Then one day late in 1968, the mystery was solved.

Paul Phillips called me into his office and informed me that Sohio's senior vice president of finance, Al Wolf, was retiring, and Paul was going to be his replacement, adding responsibilities for finance, accounting and treasury to his current duties as head of Corporate Planning.

That move was part of Sohio's succession planning, and Paul had been aware of it for quite some time. Paul was an accountant by training, but he didn't have any hands-on experience in finance. When Morgan Stanley first mentioned the idea of an "internship" to Paul, he wanted to take advantage of the opportunity himself, but his responsibilities were such that the company couldn't afford his being away for that length of time, so he asked me to go instead. Now the plan was for me to join Paul in the Finance Department and do the heavy lifting for that function.

My first assignment was to spend six months as assistant treasurer, reporting to our treasurer, Al Miller. Paul had no idea what went on in the Treasury Department—nor did I—and this was his way of finding out. I was to brief him periodically on what was going on.

The tools available to treasury departments in those days were unsophisticated, but by the same token, the issues they had to deal with back then were not complicated. Byzantine instruments such as derivatives had yet to come into vogue. I quickly realized, though, that Sohio's practices were even more simplistic than the norm. I sensed there had not been a new idea in treasury in decades, and that supposition held out the prospect that my brief tenure in the office, rather than being boring, could be kind of fun. I looked forward to dusting off the cobwebs and introducing new and better ways of doing things. As I began to explore opportunities for improvement, I was told constantly by one of the minions in the department that what I was thinking of doing was "not the way Al Nichols would have done it." Mr. Nichols was long gone from the company, and as best I could tell, he had served as treasurer around the turn of the century.

Although there were a few obvious actions that could be taken to streamline operations and improve productivity, none would increase the company's profitability in a meaningful way, with one possible exception. Treasury's primary responsibility was to manage the corporation's cash, typically around $25 million on any given day. Each day, cash was moved among our major banks to cover checks written on those accounts while leaving sufficient balances as partial compensation to the banks for our credit agreements. Any excess cash would be invested, bearing in mind, the need to have cash readily available on specific dates in the future to meet extraordinary expenses, payroll, quarterly dividends payments, and the like.

The day would start with a mid-morning call to our cash unit from those few banks where our sales receipts were deposited in lock boxes, informing us of what had been collected since the last report. The cash unit would then prepare a "bed sheet"—so called because of its size—that showed the balances in all of our major accounts, along with a tally of the expenses that needed to be paid that day. I would then let the cash unit know how much to pay out of each of the accounts, and how much to transfer from one bank account to another. Knowing how much was then available to invest, I would canvass a list of brokers to see what was being offered, and put the excess cash to work. The cash unit would then furnish me with a final version of the bed sheet, reflecting the moves that had been made. As a final step in the process, I would appear in the boss's office late morning to review the bed sheet with him so he would be comforted, knowing that, once all of the dust settled, everything would be in apple-pie order.

There was one disadvantage to our process. For two reasons, we always had significantly more money than we thought in those bank accounts where the receipts from our product sales were collected. First was the matter of "float," that is, checks we had written that had yet to be presented to the bank for payment creating a difference between the actual amount in those accounts and the balances we had recorded on our books. Second, and more significant, sales receipts were constantly being deposited in our lock box accounts, and we were always a day or so behind in knowing what our true balances were.

The solution to this dilemma was to run "red," or negative, balances, on our major accounts in amounts close to our estimates of what was really in them. (Later on, this was done automatically through "zero balance" accounts, but back then, the banks had yet to surface that idea.)

I can't claim credit for the idea of running red balances, only on executing on the idea. Before starting my job as assistant treasurer, I spent an afternoon with my predecessor getting briefed on what the job entailed. During the meeting, I asked him if there was anything he would have liked to have accomplished that he either didn't or couldn't. In response, he explained the problem of not having a timely picture of our cash balances, and as a result, we always had more money than we thought sitting in our bank accounts rather than being invested, noting the only way to deal with this was to run red balances. When I asked him why he didn't do that, he said our outside auditors, Ernst & Ernst (E&E), wouldn't permit it.

Sometime later, I was in a meeting with E&E on another matter, and after the meeting was over, I pulled aside the partner on our account and asked him why the prohibition on red bank balances existed, explaining why I wanted to do it. He said they didn't have a problem with that, but he did caution against doing it in November. Ohio assessed a personal property tax on, among other things, bank balances, and the state always based it on a day in November. For obvious reasons, they selected a different day in November every year and didn't announce the date until after the fact. Armed with E&E's approval and precaution, I was ready to change the way we did business.

I've always had an independent streak so, rather than telling my boss what I was planning to do, I proceeded on my own. The next morning, I reviewed the history of our largest bank account, National City Bank, and determined how much I could conservatively overdraw it. Then, after I got the mid-morning report on our system-wide balances, I gave instructions to the cash unit which would result in the account at National City being overdrawn by the predetermined amount. The woman responsible for carrying out these instructions was quick to let me know that something was amiss, and my plan for the day would result in the National City account being significantly in the red.

"That's fine," I said, "that's what I intended to do."

"We're not supposed to do that," she said.

"It's okay. Go ahead," I said.

After a couple more calls from the cash unit to make sure there was no misunderstanding, the final bed sheet arrived in my office. The National City account occupied a spot in the center of the page, and there in bright red was a number well into the seven figures. I moseyed over to the boss's office, laid the bed sheet in front of him for his review and comments, and waited for apoplexy to set in. I didn't have to wait long.

To avoid serious repercussions, I quickly brought Al up to date, noting that I was aware of the long-held view that our external auditors would not approve, but then explained that I had checked with E&E and found that they had no problem with it. Al clearly understood the rationale for running red balances, knowing this would generate more interest income and improve the company's profit and loss statement. He put his stamp of approval on my approach, and from that day on, running red balances became standard operating procedure. This was fun, making meaningful change where change was due.

My assignment in treasury was rapidly approaching an end, and the search for my replacement was underway. I was anxious to move on, as I had accomplished about all that I could, and the daily routine was getting boring. It's fair to say that Al was probably even more anxious to see me go. But before that happened, another incident occurred that did nothing to cause him to have second thoughts. Quite the contrary, actually.

Sohio's cash unit had two check-signing machines that processed batches of checks, imprinting a signature on each. One of the machines was getting old and unreliable, and when the company's capital budget for the coming year was compiled during the fall, I submitted a request for $8,000 for a new machine, which was included in the approved budget. Before year end, however, the old machine broke down. Dick Sparnon, who managed the cash unit, called in the repairman, who, after examining the machine, told Dick it was in bad shape and would require a major overhaul. Dick told the repairman that he was hesitant to spend the money on maintaining the old machine because we were planning to buy a new after the first of the year.

Hearing this, the repairman told Dick his company was heavily discounting new machines to reduce inventory before year-end. If we were interested, they would offer us a good price on a new machine, as well as a reasonable value for the old machine as a trade-in. Furthermore, they would bill us after the first of the year when we would have the money in our budget to pay for it. Dick relayed this information to me, and I told him to go ahead and make the purchase.

Every Monday morning, we started the week with Paul's staff meeting. In addition to me, attendees were my boss, Al, and Dick Nash, who was responsible for investor relations. A couple of weeks after my yet-to-be-authorized purchase, Paul began the meeting by telling us that Charlie Spahr had put out a notice that although the capital budgets for the coming year had been approved, concerns about the business climate had caused management to take a second look and everybody's capital budget was cut in half until further notice.

I was sitting next to my boss on the sofa in Paul's office, and upon hearing this, I chuckled, nudged him, and said, "You've got a problem."

Pressed by Paul for an explanation, I noted that the capital budget for the Finance Department—miniscule relative to the operating departments' budgets—was about $9,000, which, cut in half, would be about $4,500, and I had already spent more than that on a new check signing machine, putting us in violation of Mr. Spahr's edict. Hearing this, Paul went ballistic. I suppose, despite the meager sums involved, the last person who wanted to run afoul of budget constraints was the individual in charge of finance and accounting.

Coming off the ceiling, Paul said, "You can't do that!"

"I don't want to get into a semantics argument with you, Paul," I replied, "but I think that what you meant to say is I *shouldn't* do that rather than I can't, because I can and I did. The machine is down on the seventh floor signing checks as we speak."

I explained to Paul the reason for making the purchase early, and although we got snared by an arbitrary edict— obviously, not a defense we should use in explaining this to Charlie—it was the right thing to do and the amount involved wouldn't put the company in financial straits. I was sure Mr. Spahr would understand.

Fortunately for me, he did.

It was time for me to move on, and Paul and I began to discuss my next assignment. While my time in treasury had had its moments of fun, it did little to spark my interest in a career in finance.

22. GETTING READY FOR THE BIG ENCHILADA

Morgan Stanley advised us that, in addition to tapping public markets, we should seriously consider arranging a large private placement of debt. This would become the centerpiece of our long-term financial plan, the key to paying our share of the costs of developing the Prudhoe Bay field, constructing TAPS, building the terminal at Valdez, and commissioning the tankers to move the oil from there to the lower 48 states. In the waning months of 1974, we began making final preparations to access this huge source of funds through Finance, our newly formed Sohio/BP Trans Alaska Pipeline Finance Company. Some spade work had already been done. Senior executives from The Prudential Insurance Company of America (the Pru) and the Metropolitan Life Insurance Company (the Met)—the two biggest private placement lenders—were among those who had toured Alaska with us to get a firsthand look at our Alaskan venture.

Sam Pryor and Bob Lovejoy, attorneys from Morgan Stanley's outside counsel, Davis Polk & Wardwell, who were part of our finance team, counseled us that, for reasons relating to disclosure, we would be unable to issue debt securities in the public markets while we were engaged in the private placement process. Our cash and access to credit had to be sufficient to sustain us for the duration. The plan was to start discussions with potential lead investors in February 1975 and complete the transaction by mid-year.

Our preliminary cash flow forecast for 1975 indicated that our capital expenditures, on average, would exceed our internally generated cash by about $120 million per month, which meant we needed to have at least $600 million in cash resources to see us through the five-month private placement process. Although earlier in 1974, we had arranged $900 million of bank credit the $300 million Baldwin Agreement and the $600 million revolving line of credit—our capital expenditures for that year were on pace to reach $700 million. Since operations would generate only about $230 million, $470 million of our $900 million of bank credit would be consumed in 1974 making up the difference. That left us with a cushion of only $430 million as we headed into 1975—an amount shy of the $600 million we needed.

Although we had successfully launched our commercial paper program in 1974, that didn't increase our available credit, it only provided a less expensive alternative to borrowing from the banks. To maintain a top rating from Moody's and Standard & Poor's for our commercial paper, which was essential in our case in order to sell it, we had agreed to keep enough of our bank lines of credit unused to cover whatever amount of commercial paper was outstanding. That meant our short-term borrowings, whether from banks or from the issuance of commercial paper, could not exceed what was available under our bank lines of credit.

Recognizing that we didn't have enough cash and credit piled up to get us through the time period required to complete our private placement, we decided to issue more debt in the public market before initiating the private placement negotiations. In addition to providing extra cash, the offering would demonstrate to our counterparties in the private placement that public markets were a viable alternative, reducing the leverage they would otherwise have. At least, that was the theory.

An issue that concerned me about borrowing from insurance companies was one of the tests they would apply to determine if their loan to us constituted a "legal" investment for them. That concern came into sharp focus when we began drafting documents for our public debt offering. In order for securities to qualify as a legal investment for life insurance companies governed by New York law—and that's nearly all of them—the issuer must meet certain tests. In our case, the most severe test—and one that I knew would be a very close call for us—was coverage of fixed charges. This metric (earnings available to meet fixed charges divided by fixed charges) was designed to indicate whether a company has sufficient profits to pay its fixed obligations, primarily interest charges. Although insurance companies are allowed to invest in securities that fail to qualify as legal investments, they can do so only with a small portion of their portfolios, so insurers insist on receiving a much higher interest rate. Although paying a premium interest rate was worrisome, the limited availability of funds, if we failed the test, was an even greater concern.

The magnitude of our Alaskan project relative to Sohio's size, and the obligations we were going to incur meant we needed to convince prospective lenders to look beyond traditional metrics used to assess creditworthiness, and instead, base their judgments on the merits of the project itself. However, because the fixed charge coverage test was prescribed by law, no such objectivity could be expected on the part of the insurance companies.

Or could it?

During one of our drafting sessions, I asked the lawyers from Davis Polk & Wardwell about certain aspects of the coverage issue. They suggested I call one of their partners who was an expert on insurance law. I did, and that conversation proved to be very interesting. As it turned out, insurance companies exercised flexibility in their interpretation of the coverage of fixed charge test. They were a bit more generous in that regard when they were eager to make an investment. Other times, they might be more rigid, if, say, they wanted to avoid honoring a commitment they had made.

Turning to the issue of methodology, I mentioned to the lawyer that I was able to come up with more than one way to arrive at certain information used to calculate the coverage ratio on a pro forma basis and was interested in convincing the insurance companies to accept the approach that produced the most favorable answer for us. He told me the best way to accomplish my objective would be to get our outside auditors to sign off on our preferred approach while examining our financial statements for the upcoming public offering.

Following up on that advice, I met with Dick Popeney and Hugh Mullen, Ernst & Ernst's partners on our account, and walked them through how I proposed to determine Sohio's coverage of fixed charges. I was careful to make note of the alternate ways of calculating the ratio, which I'm sure they understood, all the while giving a strong rationale for my way of doing it. Concerned that they might start thinking about the possibility of incurring additional liabilities, I shied away from telling them the real reason I was so passionate about this issue. It was a lengthy meeting and there was a lot of discussion, but they finally agreed to go along with my methodology.

The unique structure of Sohio/BP Trans Alaska Pipeline Finance Company, with BP being part of it, made getting all of the approvals for Finance's first public debt offering a lengthy and cumbersome ordeal. BP had to solicit certain approvals from the UK government and the Bank of England. We started drafting documents on August 30, 1974, and after drafting two amendments to the registration statement to respond to questions raised by the SEC, we finally were ready to price the offering and go to press. In the wee hours of the morning of December 4, as we were putting the final touches on the offering prospectus, the two young associates from Ernst & Ernst who were reviewing the document told me a mistake had been made in the calculation of the coverage of fixed charges.

Apparently, Dick and Hugh had neglected to tell the associates they had agreed to my methodology instead of the more traditional approach the associates were using. My efforts to convince them that my numbers were correct, and that E&E was on board with my approach, fell on deaf ears. Out of exasperation, I picked up the phone and called Hugh. Being jarred out of a sound sleep at two o'clock in the morning is one thing. Having a maniac on the other end of the line screaming at you is another. After I was sure I had

Hugh's undivided attention, I handed the phone to one of the associates. Soon after that, we finished the prospectus and prepared the filing package to be sent to the SEC in the morning. I headed home, having established a good position for us on the matter of coverage of fixed charges. The next day, Finance sold $250 million of debentures maturing in 1999 and paying 9¾ percent interest.

Within a week of offering the 25-year debentures, David Goodman told us there was an appetite in the marketplace for shorter-term investments. Would we be interested? We had raised enough cash and credit to cover our needs during the time we would be blocked out of the public markets, but with nothing to spare. If the private placement negotiations dragged on longer than we had planned, halting the proceedings and jumping back into the public market probably was not an alternative. Lenders would know we had been unsuccessful in our private placement efforts and would, rightly or wrongly, assume those potential lenders had learned something about our project that caused them to back away. We decided a little more cushion wouldn't hurt, and our documents were fresh. So another crank of the printing press, and on January 29, 1975, Finance issued $250 million of 8⅝ percent notes maturing in eight years. Our 67.8 percent of the proceeds from the two offerings swelled our coffers by $339 million before expenses.

Finally, we were set to take on the insurance companies.

23. THE SAGA BEGINS

Months of work went into preparing the private placement offering memorandum. It was a team effort. Paul and I worked closely with David Goodman to sculpt the unique approach to be taken. David's partners chimed in along the way. And the members of our finance team labored intensely, preparing all the documents.

But the driving force was David, whose creativity and tenacity made it happen. In the midst of our private placement preparations, David took a couple of weeks off to vacation at his Eleuthera Island home in the Bahamas. He was not the type of person to let vacation stop him from participating, so on a regular basis he called the finance team to relay ideas that had occurred to him while basking on the beach. Generally, David's ideas were good ones. But most of the ones being phoned in from the Bahamas didn't make a lot of sense. Concerned and bemused, the team started telling David to be sure to remember to wear his pith helmet when out in the noon-day sun.

By the end of February, we completed the offering memorandum, over 200 pages, and, including lengthy appendices, nearly three inches thick. It laid out for prospective participants excruciating detail on the terms of the offering, a description of the project, Sohio's plan for financing its share of it, pertinent background information about Sohio and BP, as well as financial statements for each. Among other things, the appendices contained, uniquely, drafts of the indenture, as well as Sohio and BP Pipelines' note purchase agreements, setting forth the covenants or restrictions that would apply to the borrowers.

Designing the covenants that would apply to Sohio took a lot of creative thought. They had to provide adequate protection for the lenders, but they also had to insure that Sohio would have the flexibility to see the project through to completion. Although such matters would be subject to negotiation, we concluded that we would have a leg up by presenting prospective lenders our thoughts on the covenants rather than taking the traditional approach of developing them jointly after commitments were in hand, which is why comprehensive drafts of the indenture and the note purchase agreements were included in the offering memorandum.

Aside from the numerous covenants that are normal in transactions of this type, there were two that were unique to our situation. David Goodman devised a couple of complex restrictions to maintain the delicate balance between lender and borrower that we were trying to achieve. First, in line with our "project financing" concept, he came up with the notion of a "project allowable" limitation on indebtedness that Sohio could incur, as opposed to the more normal debt-to-equity ratio restriction. The project allowable limited Sohio's borrowings for Prudhoe Bay field development, TAPS, tankers, and a West Coast-Midcontinent pipeline to move North Slope crude oil from California to Texas to $3.75 billion. Indebtedness, apart from our Alaskan project, would be allowed up to a maximum of $700 million.

The second restriction David conjured up pertained to the rate Sohio could draw down funds under the private placement. To complete our Alaskan project, we would need to secure funds from sources other than the private placement. Given our precarious financial condition, we felt it important to assure the private placement participants that we would find and use funds from these other sources in the same proportion as monies coming from them. Otherwise, they might be concerned that Sohio would draw down all of the private placement funds, fail to secure financing from other sources, be unable to finish the project, and leave them with a potential disaster on their hands. To achieve this balance, David proposed a series of quarterly takedowns, along with a "takedown formula" that would keep a proper alignment between funding sources. In order to take down 50 percent of the private placement, for example, Sohio would have to represent that its cumulative expenditures for the project amounted to at least 50 percent of the estimated total cost to complete it. This limitation was an innovative way to provide the comfort that prospective lenders would be seeking.

The size of the proposed offering was set at $750 million with a maturity of twenty years and an interest rate of ten percent. In March, offering memorandums were presented to the Pru and the Met. Each insurance firm was asked to consider being the lead lender, committing to at least a $250 million participation.

The Pru was first to respond. In early April, a representative called David Goodman to express his concerns, saying the interest rate was too low, the commitment fee paid on funds committed but not drawn down was too low, and the maturity of twenty years was too long. Prudential didn't comment on the covenants. The call was brief, and its tone was such that Morgan Stanley felt there was a complete lack of interest on the part of the Pru.

Fortunately, we still had the Met as our fallback. In late April, the Met called Morgan Stanley and said they were very concerned about Sohio's financial situation and unsure that oil prices would be high enough to render the project economically viable. The risks were too great to justify making the investment.

In response to Morgan Stanley's question about what could be done to make the deal attractive, the Met replied, "There are so many problems, challenges, and uncertainties associated with this whole thing that it is absolutely impossible for you to do anything to make this attractive to us. We honestly have no interest whatsoever."

That was disappointing, to say the least.

|||

There were, indeed, uncertainties aplenty. Under the Trans-Alaska Pipeline Authorization Act, any oil moved through TAPS could not be exported. The oil industry had always done—and still does—an excellent job of moving crude oil from where it was produced to refineries around the globe in a very efficient manner. Transportation economies were accomplished by shortening the supply lines through buying, selling, and trading oil. Absent the export prohibition, some of the oil from Prudhoe Bay might be shipped to Japan in exchange for Middle East oil being sent to US refineries on the East Coast. That swap would be less expensive than shipping Prudhoe Bay oil from Valdez, Alaska to the East Coast, and Middle East oil to Japan.

As is too often the case, political optics trumped logic. The export prohibition was put in place, and with that the people at Sohio who would be responsible for selling or trading our Prudhoe Bay oil studied the shape of the US market for crude and the alternatives for getting our Alaskan oil there. Refinery locations and their capacities—an indicator of demand for crude oil—were a couple of key considerations. Also, crude oils vary in their properties. Some crudes are heavy; some are light. Some are sour, that is, high in sulfur content. Others are sweet. Refineries are designed to process crude oil with certain properties, and their raw material needs are met by mixing crudes together to produce a blend they can handle. Understanding how such constraints impacted the market for Prudhoe Bay crude oil also was important.

The closest US market for Prudhoe Bay crude oil was the West Coast. Taking into account the total refining capacity on the West Coast, and then factoring in indigenous production of crude oil as well as imports that wouldn't be displaced by Prudhoe Bay crude—Indonesian Sweet crude, which is very low in sulfur and needed to mix with high sulfur crudes, and Canadian crude shipped to Puget Sound refineries designed specifically to process it—it was clear there would be more Prudhoe Bay crude produced than the West Coast could absorb, making it necessary to transport the surplus to US markets east of the Rocky Mountains.

Unfortunately, the only way to get it there would be to ship it by tanker through the Panama Canal to ports on either the Gulf Coast or the East Coast, and then through existing pipeline systems to inland refineries. The tankers picking up the oil in Valdez would be too large to transit the Panama Canal, making it necessary to offload the cargo into smaller tankers—"Panamax" vessels that can pass through the canal—an extremely costly and inefficient proposition. Sohio concluded that, instead, a West Coast–Midcontinent pipeline would be the most direct and economic method for transporting our Alaskan crude oil east of the Rockies.

Sohio engaged William Brothers Engineering Company to examine alternate routes for a West Coast–Midcontinent pipeline. Two routes and their related port facilities were studied: a northern route originating in the Puget Sound area and a southern route coming out of California. Their analysis produced a promising option that would utilize 670 miles of an existing gas transmission line, largely owned by the El Paso Company, to transport crude oil from Long Beach, California to a terminal near Midland, Texas. From there, crude oil could be shipped through existing pipeline systems to refineries in the mid-continent area.

In May of 1975, Sohio reached a preliminary agreement with El Paso to convert one of its main gas transmission lines running from the Permian Basin area in West Texas westward to the California-Arizona border to an oil pipeline. Docks and terminal facilities would have to be constructed in Long Beach, and a new pipeline would have to be laid from there to the western end of the El Paso line. Another new line would be needed to connect the eastern end of the El Paso line to the existing terminal in Midland. The system would be about 1,000 miles long. We dubbed the pipeline PacTex. We would need Federal Power Commission approval to enable El Paso to "abandon" its line from gas transmission service, permits and approvals from local and state agencies in California and Texas, as well as dealing with environmental groups that were sure to oppose the project. Assuming engineering started in 1975 and the approvals could be obtained in two years, PacTex could be operational by mid-1978.

A number of unknowns complicated our financial planning. Until the preliminary design was done, we would lack a good handle on the cost to build PacTex. We were pretty sure, however, that it would be less than the cost of a newly constructed line, which we estimated to be about $1 billion. While we had good reason to believe other companies would be interested in becoming part owners of PacTex, no one was willing to sign up until we had the approvals in hand, so we didn't know how much of the line we would ultimately own. Nor did we know what kind of ownership structure the participants might agree to. The best we could do was pencil in some "soft" numbers in the 1976-1977 timeframe, representing our best guesses of our share of the cost of constructing PacTex. Of more immediate concern, we estimated it would cost us in the neighborhood of $30 million for PacTex activities, prior to receiving the necessary approvals.

III

A financial crisis brewing in the State of Alaska added to the list of uncertainties we were dealing with. After the Prudhoe Bay discovery was announced, the oil industry was eager to step up exploration activities on the North Slope. Taking advantage of the oil companies' appetite for more leases to explore, in September 1969, Alaska auctioned off 164 tracts, collecting $900 million merely for the rights to explore for oil.

Like most governments are prone to do, Alaska ramped up its spending to match its new-found riches. Believing that income from the state's 12.5 percent royalty from production of Prudhoe Bay crude oil would commence with the startup of TAPS in 1972, it saw no need to practice fiscal constraint. As delays in the startup of TAPS delayed the receipt of royalty payments, rather than reducing spending, Alaska looked for other sources of revenue, and the oil companies represented an attractive target.

The solution Governor William Eagan came up with in May of 1975 was to impose a tax on oil reserves on the North Slope, which would be in effect in 1976 and 1977. We estimated that this tax—a new and totally unexpected cost, and an egregious one, at that—would cost Sohio $240 to $300 million.

Because the tax was levied only on companies that had reserves on the North Slope, it was deemed to be discriminatory. A consortium of companies with leases on the North Slope threatened to sue. The state and the oil companies finally compromised by agreeing that the taxes paid would be creditable against future severance taxes levied on oil production. In essence, the "tax" was an interest free-loan to the state.

III

In assessing the fact that our private placement had been rejected by both the Pru and the Met, we kept coming back to the fact that it was to be the centerpiece of our financial plan. The Met was clearly not an option. Reflecting on the Pru's criticism of our proposal, we thought having Morgan Stanley go back to them with better financial terms was worth a try. Interest rates had inched up since we started the process, so we decided to propose a higher rate and a choice of maturities. With this change, the Pru was interested— very interested. As the largest life insurance company in the United States and the largest institutional investor, Prudential decided it should play a leading role in such a vital project as TAPS if the credit considerations proved satisfactory.

During follow-on discussions among Sohio, Morgan Stanley and James Toren, a Prudential vice president and one of three key Pru executives assigned to the transaction, we agreed to raise the interest rate to 10⅝ percent to attract a large number of lenders. Then Toren suggested we consider increasing the amount we were seeking from $750 million to something on the order of $1 billion to $1.75 billion.

Another billion was indeed impressive and would go a long way toward convincing the world at large that, as far as financing the pipeline was concerned, we were going to get the job done. With that in mind we persuaded Sohio's board of directors that it made good sense to raise as much money in this offering as we could and we opted to increase the amount we would go after to $1.75 billion.

In late May, the Pru committed to take $250 million, which would be the largest loan it had ever made. Morgan Stanley then presented the proposal to other investors, offering a choice of maturities: either an 18-year note due in 1993 or a 23-year note due in 1998. By early July, aided by a slight easing of interest rates in the credit markets, seventy five additional lenders signed up, bringing the total commitments to the sought-after amount. Like the Pru, for most of them, this would be the largest investment they ever made. And the $1.75 billion private placement would be the largest ever, nearly three times the size of the previous biggest private placement transaction.

From there, it was merely a matter of negotiating the covenants and drafting the documents.

Shouldn't take too long, should it?

24. Finance? No, Thanks

P aul and I had agreed that my stint as assistant treasurer would last for six months, after which I would
be given other duties within the Finance Department,
once again reporting directly to him. As the time for me to
change jobs was approaching, Paul and I began to discuss
my next assignment. He was proposing to promote me to a
newly created position, manager, financial planning. As we
sketched out what my duties would be, I became convinced
the job would be even more mundane than my assignment
in treasury.

After thinking it over, I told him, "Sorry Paul, I just don't
want the job,"

Paul was not happy. He had arranged for me to work at
Morgan Stanley to prepare me to assume this role in finance,
and he felt strongly that I was obliged to accept the job.

"I don't have to. I'm simply not interested in finance,"
I said to him. "There isn't enough to do to fill up an eight-
hour day, and the job just isn't challenging enough for me."

Paul then told me the company planned to raise $100
million dollars in a public offering and there wasn't anybody
else in the company who could handle the responsibility.

"Okay, here's the deal," I said, "I'll take the job. I'll manage the offering for you. But you have to promise me the day
we close, you'll find something more interesting for me to do
outside of finance."

"Deal!" he said.

Motivated to get the offering behind me so that I could
move on to something more exciting, I began laying the
groundwork for it. The former head of Sohio's Finance

Department, Al Wolf, had come from F. S. Moseley, and that firm had served as Sohio's investment banker, even though there hadn't been a need for one. In the 1960s, changing investment banking relationships was not done casually.

Because of my relationship with Morgan Stanley, and more important, my belief that we needed stronger representation for a deal as large as $100 million, we decided to switch investment bankers. As a first step, I spoke with Morgan Stanley to make sure that they were interested in leading the underwriting. Although the firm had been giving us advice on acquisitions for some time, I knew they were very selective when it came to taking on clients.

Thankfully, the firm agreed to do it. What's more, recognizing the sensitivity associated with dropping F. S. Moseley as our investment banker, Morgan Stanley volunteered to allow Moseley to co-manage the offering, an unusual concession on its part.

The next step was to give F. S. Moseley the bad news, tempered somewhat by the co-management sop that Morgan Stanley had offered for this one deal. Paul and I arranged for a morning meeting with Jack Stubbs, the head of F. S. Moseley. We flew into Boston the night before the meeting, had a late dinner, and then over drinks, wrestled with how we were going to broach the subject with Mr. Stubbs. I suggested to Paul that we put the onus for firing Moseley on me. We would tell Jack that I spent a summer interning with Morgan Stanley, and that I had a good relationship with the firm, unlike F. S. Moseley, who I didn't know, and that relationship provided a level of comfort that was extremely important to me.

Paul didn't think this was the best approach, so we didn't settle on anything, deciding that we would wing it when we got there.

In the morning when we arrived, Jack's secretary informed me that I needed to call my office. I went into a conference room to make my call as Paul was being ushered into Jack's office.

When I finished my call, I was led into Jack's office, and after I said "Hello" to Jack, he looked at me and said, "So, you're the guy who had an internship at Morgan Stanley?"

I could only assume that while I was preoccupied with my call, Paul had switched gears and decided to tell Jack this was all my doing.

So, I said, "Yes, I did," and proceeded to explain my rationale for making the switch to Morgan Stanley, ending by telling him about the firm's gesture to ease the transition by having Moseley co-manage the first underwriting. Then, thanking Jack for his time, we got out of there.

Out on the street, I asked Paul why he had changed his mind about how to break the news to Jack.

"I didn't," he said. "We were having a cordial conversation about nothing in general, waiting for you to join the meeting. What followed was a complete surprise to me."

The best that Paul and I could figure out was that Jack, not knowing why we were coming to see him but suspicious of our intent, had started calling around, and somehow or other, found out about my relationship with Morgan Stanley. Despite the sudden turn of events, it did serve to keep Paul and me from hemming and hawing, enabling us instead to get right to the point.

With that awkward situation out of the way, I began working in earnest with Morgan Stanley to complete the offering as soon as possible so that I could head off to bigger and better things.

And that is exactly when fate intervened and Sohio started its negotiations with BP. Suddenly, my job was going to be very challenging indeed.

Little did I know just how challenging.

25. KEEPING YOUR EYE ON THE BALL

With $1.75 billion in private placement commitments in hand, conversations with the lead lender, the Pru, turned to the question of who would draft the agreements. A time-honored business principle: when you're involved in a transaction, you're better off "controlling the pencil," that is, preparing the documents governing the deal. The other side gets to comment on what is presented, but you're well ahead of the game if they have to respond to what you put on the table rather than the other way around.

We suggested that it made sense for our lawyers to write the documents, having already done extensive drafting while preparing the offering memorandum. But the Pru had no interest in that and invoked another time-honored business principle, the Golden Rule: "He who has the gold, rules." The Pru's outside counsel, who was not held in high esteem by our side, was assigned the task of preparing the documents.

The day the first draft of the purchase agreement was to arrive, the hard-core members of our finance team—David Goodman, Sam Pryor, Bob Lovejoy, George Dunn, and I—gathered in one of Sohio's conference rooms to review it.

Although it was a lengthy document—about one inch-thick—we decided everyone should take a quick run through it to get an overview. After that, we'd all plow through it, page by page, to discuss and record the changes we felt needed to be made.

It didn't take long to realize that the document was hopelessly garbled and unduly restrictive. Soon, the moans of despair began.

"Oh, my God, look at this...."

"Can you believe that...?"

The wailing and gnashing of teeth went on for about a half hour until I decided I needed to get the group under some semblance of control and refocused on the big picture. I flipped to the back of the document and said, "Hey guys, what's this?"

"Where are you?" someone asked. I gave him the page number.

Everybody turned to that page and, puzzled, one of them said, "That's the signature page."

"Does that mean if I sign on the dotted line, we get the money?" I asked rhetorically.

From the expressions on their faces, I knew it wasn't necessary to remind them what our overarching objective was. I acknowledged the document needed a lot of work, but given our cash situation, we couldn't let that get in the way of closing on the transaction as soon as possible. Many years later, Bob Lovejoy wrote me a warm letter telling me he was leaving Davis Polk & Wardwell and the practice of law to join Lazard Freres as an investment banker. He recounted this incident, along with others, ending with words of praise, "Now, that's keeping your eye on the ball."

Given the complexities of the private placement and the issues that needed to be sorted out, face-to-face meetings to negotiate terms and conditions satisfactory to both sides would prove necessary. For me, that meant heading off on Monday mornings to Prudential's home office in Newark, New Jersey where I would meet up with David Goodman and Bob Lovejoy to spend the day engaged in endless discussions with a dozen or so individuals representing the seventy six investors in the deal. Art Carlson, general investment manager for the Pru, was the lead spokesman for the other side. But all of the other representatives were from firms making their largest investments ever and, typically in most of their deals, they were the lead investors and did things their own way.

Getting a consensus from that group was not easy.

The project allowable debt and the debt-takedown schedule and formula—two items that were vitally important to us—were never challenged. But there were numerous other details that had to be ironed out, preventing us from reaching agreement with the lenders in a timely manner. In some instances, the differences that needed to be reconciled were among the lenders themselves. One of the most difficult issues was establishing the conditions to be imposed upon us, if not met, that would enable lenders to get out of their commitments. Quarterly takedowns of specified amounts were scheduled until July 1, 1977. Within limits designed to ensure that sufficient funds would be provided to us in time to meet our needs, each lender was allowed to designate when they wanted to put up their share, or some portion of it. Those lenders who opted to put in funds early on were concerned that those coming in later, should they be so inclined for one reason or another, might have an excuse not to participate if the conditions that we had to meet at the time of each takedown were too stringent and we were unable to meet them. Losing their participation could result in us not having sufficient funds to complete our project which could leave those who had already invested in a world of hurt. On the other hand, if the conditions were too lax, the lenders coming in later might be obligated to invest good money after bad.

Complicating this debate was the matter of the coverage of fixed charges test used to determine whether or not an investment is legal under the New York laws governing insurance companies. Some insurance companies interpreted this requirement to mean the test had to be met when a commitment was made. Others interpreted this same requirement to mean the test had to be met when funds were actually drawn down. Because Sohio's financial condition, as measured by this metric, would surely worsen as additional borrowings occurred, it was not unreasonable to assume that, as time passed, we might fail the fixed charge coverage test. To address this, there was a lot of jockeying to get those with the view that the test applied when the commitment was made to come in later, since meeting the test would be moot at that time, and vice-versa. This impasse was one of the last issues to be put to bed, but finally, in early November, all of the lenders were satisfied, not only with their own positions, but with the positions of all of the others in the syndicate.

A couple of other rather bizarre issues cropped up in the course of finalizing the agreements. First, the financings done through Sohio/BP Trans Alaska Pipeline Finance Inc. were structured as a two-step proposition. Finance would borrow the money and then use the proceeds to purchase debt securities from their respective pipeline subsidiaries, Sohio Pipeline Company and BP Pipelines Inc., thereby transferring the borrowings to where the funds were needed. This approach technically violated the Federal Reserve Board's Regulation T, which governs the amount of credit brokerage firms and dealers can extend to customers for the purchase of securities on margin. In the case of our private placement, Morgan Stanley, as broker dealer, was arranging credit for Finance to purchase securities, something that was prohibited by Regulation T. To legitimize our transaction, Davis Polk & Wardwell, on behalf of Morgan Stanley, asked the Board of Governors of the Federal Reserve System to agree that Regulation T did not apply in our case, given the rationale for the two-step approach being used. The board concurred.

The second issue was not quite as abstruse. Someone discovered that firms with "finance" in their names cannot qualify to do business in the State of New York. Go figure. The private placement lenders insisted that the borrower, Sohio/BP Trans Alaska Pipeline Finance Inc., be qualified to do business in New York, in case they found it necessary to take us to court to remedy any grievance they might have. So we changed the name of the borrowing entity to Sohio/BP Trans Alaska Pipeline Capital Inc.

Although our negotiations over mind-numbing details seemed to go on forever, there were occasional light moments. One came while we were discussing the restrictions to be imposed on Sohio's ability to sell an interest in our Prudhoe

Bay crude oil reserves or dedicate a portion of our production in the form of the advance sale of crude oil—either one
of which would erode the lenders' collateral. We had asked
for a limited ability to do some of this and had proposed a
modest carve-out to the restriction on those types of transactions. Don Schenck, Prudential's general counsel, as part
of his due diligence, had become aware of our Columbia
and Baldwin agreements. Concerned that we might show
the same kind of ingenuity to use the carve-out to the lenders' detriment, he argued against giving us any leeway whatsoever. He and I debated the matter at length, and I think the
points I was making in support of our request were proving
persuasive to the others in the room.

Finally, out of frustration, he turned to Art Carlson and
said, "You know, Art, if you agree with what John wants
to do, Sohio can produce its Prudhoe Bay crude oil, ship
it down the pipeline, and sell it in the marketplace ..." at
which point I interjected, "and that's exactly what we intend
to do, Art, because if we don't there isn't a chance in hell
you'll get paid back."

That comment broke up the room. More important, it
won the day. We got our carve-out.

Unfortunately, the few opportunities for fun and games
didn't make up for the delays in reaching an agreement and
getting the deal closed. Weeks of negotiations morphed into
months.

26. MURPHY WAS AN OPTIMIST

July 1975, the original completion date of our private placement had come and gone, and we were still struggling to agree on certain terms and conditions. As long as we were embroiled in these negotiations, we were precluded from offering debt securities to the public.

But we could sell stock, and in addition to being a token offering to the rating gods, this would provide us with a much needed infusion of cash. Excluding interest related to funds borrowed for construction, which was becoming a significant amount and increasing rapidly, our investment in the oil field and the pipeline during 1975 was estimated to be $340 million and $770 million, respectively, for a total of $1.1 billion, contrasted to our expectations that operations would generate only about $240 million during the year.

We began preparing to sell two million shares of The Standard Oil Company common stock. The 1969 agreement with BP, whereby we acquired all its interests in the United States in exchange for a stock interest in Sohio, had an anti-dilution provision that entitled BP to purchase 54 percent of any new stock to be offered for sale, leaving us with 920,000 shares that we could sell to the public.

From the standpoint of price, the timing was good. Our stock had hit a low of about $44 per share in the first quarter of the year, but by early August, it was selling close to $80. Preparations went smoothly, and we satisfied the SEC's comments and questions on our offering documents by early September. All systems were go when Murphy's law came into play.

Captain Edward A. Murphy's most famous law says that, "If anything can go wrong, it will."

Based on my experience with our Alaskan venture, I judged Captain Murphy to be a wide-eyed optimist.

III

In addition to drilling 130 production wells and building miles and miles of pipeline to connect those wells with flow stations, other processing and ancillary equipment had to be installed at Prudhoe Bay: base camps to house personnel, power stations with enough electricity generating capacity for a small city, large gathering centers for separating natural gas and water from the oil that's produced, and huge compressors to re-inject the natural gas back into the reservoirs. Typically, this gas would be flared, but the federal pipeline permit prohibited flaring, requiring reinjection instead as a conservation measure.

Conditions were harsh on the North Slope. February was the coldest month, with average temperatures ranging from a low of minus 22 degrees Fahrenheit to a high of minus 12 degrees, and temperatures of 50 or 60 degrees below zero were not unheard of. With the wind chill factor, on occasion it felt even colder. To make matters worse, it was totally dark for 65 days in the winter. Summer was better. July was the warmest month, with average temperatures of 33 to 45 degrees Fahrenheit. Opposite the winter, the sun did not set for 65 days, but outsized black flies made for miserable sun bathing.

The harsh Arctic conditions wreaked havoc with productivity, which meant that construction on the North Slope would be extremely difficult and expensive. A decision was made to prefabricate facilities in modular form in the Lower 48 and ship them to Prudhoe Bay for final assembly. The modules would be transported to Prudhoe Bay on barges.

As the summer of 1975 drew to a close, prefabricated modules were placed on 47 barges, some of them the size of a football field. The larger modules weighed as much as 1,300

tons and stood as tall as nine stories. The barges rendez-
voused in Seattle with a number of tug boats for their trek to
Prudhoe Bay, a trip that had become an annual undertaking
as a means of delivering construction supplies to the North
Slope. The armada proceeded to Point Barrow, the north-
ernmost point on the route, where the barges waited for the
Arctic Ocean ice to break up, something it does every year,
and then for the winds to blow the ice offshore. Once that
happened, there would be a six-to-eight week window during which the barges could make a mad dash for Prudhoe
Bay. But the ice didn't break up. And if the barges didn't get
to Prudhoe Bay, the start of production would most likely be
delayed a year, straining Sohio's already precarious financial
condition.

With this uncertainty, it was impossible to proceed with
our stock offering. And we were rapidly running out of cash.

The barges got within 300 miles of Prudhoe by early
September. Ice breakers were brought in to help. When it
became apparent that there wouldn't be enough time for all
of the barges to make it in, the ones carrying smaller modules were sent back to Seward, where they were unloaded
and transported to Prudhoe Bay by rail, truck, or air.

We anxiously monitored developments and weather
reports on a daily basis. David Lybarger, who worked in
Sohio's Exploration and Production Department, was
our company's liaison with those individuals in charge
of developing the oil field. One of David's "advisors" on
local weather conditions was an old member of the Inupiat
Eskimo tribe living in Point Barrow. He told David the ice
always broke up, and he assured us it would break up once
again this year.

But no such luck.

Eventually, with the help of ice breakers, 11 barges carrying the larger modules managed to get within a mile-and-
a-half of Prudhoe Bay, when they got stuck in the ice for
the winter. A mile-and-a-half was, as the saying goes, close
enough for horseshoes, government work, and our needs at
the time. All we had to do now was build a gravel causeway
out to the barges and unload them. Thank God, gravel was

plentiful in Alaska and the water in that part of the Arctic Ocean was shallow!

III

With the crisis behind us and reasonably confident that startup would not be delayed, we proceeded with our offering, and on October 2nd, Morgan Stanley led the underwriting effort. We closed a week later, netting $136.5 million, which was about 10 percent less than we had hoped for. But as they say, don't mess with Mother Nature, particularly when she has Murphy on her side.

Getting the permits to build the causeway to the barges took a couple of months. The causeway was built over the winter months by cutting out huge blocks of ice and filling in the gaps with gravel. In addition to carrying prefabricated modules, the barges came equipped with gigantic crawlers to transport the modules to their ultimate locations. These crawlers were a by-product of the US space program, designed by NASA to move rockets to their launching pads. Slowly. Very slowly.

27. BALING WIRE AND DUCT TAPE

T
hose days before we completed the much-needed stock offering, when the barges were stuck in the ice, our negotiations on the private placement were stuck in the mud, and our lines of credit were close to being fully used, were dark days indeed.

At a point in time during that grim period, our treasurer, Al Miller, called to tell me, "a gentleman named H. F. B. 'Duke' Johnson from the Bank of Nova Scotia" was in the his office. Duke was making cold calls on prospective customers throughout the United States, something that seemed to me to an exercise in futility because most times people were out of the office or otherwise occupied. But cold calling was a tactic some bankers still used, and it was fortuitous that Duke showed up that day.

Al explained to me that Canadian banks, unlike banks chartered in the US, did not have legal lending limits and preferred to go it alone in credit arrangements rather than be part of a syndicate. Further, he explained, the Bank of Nova Scotia was a large institution, capable of making big loans. He thought I might want to meet with Duke.

Boy, did I! "Send him up," I said.

Al told Duke that I might be interested in exploring the possibility of a revolving credit agreement and pointed him in my direction. Duke and I spent all of two minutes exchanging pleasantries when he raised the subject of establishing a revolving credit arrangement with his bank. We had no relationship with Duke's bank, and I was unsure how much credit they would be willing to extend to us. A $100 million line would tide us over until we closed on the private placement. So I told Duke that, yes, we had been considering increasing our credit lines, and that I had something in the neighborhood of $200 million in mind.

"Why don't we talk about a $100 million, for starters," Duke said, without hesitation.

I agreed and gave Duke an overview of Sohio, focusing on our Alaskan project. Having been frequent visitors to the public securities market, we always had fresh offering documents available. I handed Duke a copy of our most recent one. He said he would go back to his hotel, read it, and then give me a call.

Duke called later that afternoon. He was prepared to recommend that his bank provide us with a credit facility along the lines we had discussed. He told me he was going to cancel the rest of his trip and head back to headquarters in Toronto to refine his credit analysis and review his proposal with the higher-ups in his organization.

Friday afternoon Duke called to tell me his management had approved his recommendation. But because of the size of the credit facility, he also needed the approval of his board of directors which he was confident wouldn't be a problem. As fate would have it, his board was meeting the following Monday, and Sohio's board, which also had to approve the transaction, was scheduled to meet on Tuesday.

How lucky could you get?

Duke called me Monday afternoon to report that his board had approved Sohio for a $100 million revolving line of credit. He was a little on edge. He had up until that point spent less than 30 minutes with me, and now he was out on a limb, depending on somebody he didn't really know to follow through on what he said he was going to do. I told him we were on the board's agenda, and assured him the board would approve the transaction when they met the following morning. I said I would call as soon as I got out of the meeting.

At times it was more difficult than others to make the sale, but I never had Sohio's board reject any of my recommendations. Given our perilous financial situation, this was a no brainer. No way would they say no. And by mid-morning Tuesday, I reported to Duke, the credit line was a go. He suggested he fly to Cleveland in the morning to work on the documentation. Having nothing more important to do, I agreed.

The next morning, Duke arrived in my office with the vice chairman of the Bank of Nova Scotia, Peter Godsoe. George Dunn joined us to aid in the drafting and before lunchtime, the credit agreement had been signed—one week to the day of Duke's cold call on Sohio.

28. FOUR FLUSHER'S FINALE

Winter was coming, and I was on another Monday morning flight to Prudential's offices in Newark, New Jersey to continue negotiations on the private placement. Despite everybody's hard work and good intentions, we weren't making any progress. Some obstacles seemed insurmountable. The financial covenants were complex because Sohio needed the flexibility to fund completion of its Alaskan project while adequately protecting the lenders, some of whom were making their largest-ever investments, including lead investor, the Pru.

We started this process in February, thinking we would be done by July. We assumed the funds we had raised in public markets in late 1974 and early 1975, along with sizable lines of credit, would be sufficient—with some room to spare—to cover our expenditures until we closed on the private placement. But as the negotiations continued through the summer and into the fall, our cash pile dwindled, and we found it necessary to seek additional funds to stay afloat. We had pulled a lot of rabbits out of the hat, but I was fresh out of ideas for where to turn next.

The more I worked with David Goodman, the stronger our relationship became. I was able to have blunt, candid conversations with him without creating problems between us. As the months dragged on with no end in sight for our private placement, I would pick up the phone and yell at him, reminding him time and again of the dire straits we were in financially and the need to get closure on our transaction. Eventually, I told David, rather than repeating myself, I would give each of my speeches a number and when I called him, I would simply say, for example, "David. This is John calling to deliver speech number one," and he would know what I meant. While venting my spleen in this way made me feel better for a short period of time, it didn't solve the problem.

Staring out of the plane window, I tried to think of a way to break the logjam. I mulled over the idea of telling everybody we were calling the whole thing off. That would get their attention! I had played a little poker in my day and had run a four-flusher's bluff or two, but never with stakes as high or a hand as lousy as the one I had been dealt. But it was all I could come up with, and I decided it was worth a try. Nobody at Sohio was aware of what I was planning to do. I figured that if my bluff backfired, they could claim the pressure had gotten to me, that I had completely lost my mind, fire me for cause—stupidity—then swoop in and pick up the pieces.

When I arrived at the Pru's offices, I pulled David Goodman aside and told him I was going to call off the deal because we weren't making any progress. Sohio was running out of time and money, and I needed to figure out something else to do that would address our problem.

He said something like, "You can't do that."

And I told him, "Just watch."

The meeting started with the usual cast of characters around the table—15 or 20 lawyers, representatives from a number of large investors, Pru representatives, David and I—and I gave my speech. Everyone was stunned. David said he had just heard of my decision that morning and had called an emergency meeting with his partners to discuss the situation, concluding by telling everyone to sit tight.

David and I headed to Morgan Stanley's headquarters in mid-town Manhattan and made a beeline for Dick Fisher's office. Dick had been a senior project leader when I did my internship at Morgan Stanley, and I had gotten to know him back then. He now was in charge of the fixed income side of the business. David and I explained to Dick what was going on and why David had called for a partners' meeting. As David and Dick started out the door, Dick invited me to join the meeting. I knew everybody who was going to be there, and I might as well hear things firsthand.

All of the partners who were in town gathered around a table to wait for John Young, Morgan Stanley's partner in charge, to arrive. I'm guessing Mr. Young was about 80 years old and had suffered one or two heart attacks, but he was extremely energetic and decisive. He crashed through the doors, pulled up a chair, sat down and asked David what was going on. David explained the private placement negotiations had been dragging on for months, that we weren't making any progress, that I had to find a way to keep money flowing into Sohio, so I was calling off the private placement.

"If we don't get this deal done, and done fast, it's John's ass," David concluded.

Larry Parker, one of David's partners responded "If we don't get this deal done, and done fast, it's your ass, David."

John Young threw back his head, roared with laughter and said, "Aha, fungible assholes."

He then turned serious and got down to business. He asked David which investors had problems with the deal and what the issues were. David had organized the problems by type and they fell into roughly four categories. He reviewed the various sticking points and then referred to a list of ten of the top institutional investors who had refused to compromise on one or more of these matters. A debate ensued. A course of action was agreed upon and David was assigned to carry it out. The meeting was then adjourned.

Starting at the top of his list, David contacted each of the recalcitrant investors and told them if they wanted to participate, they had to do it Sohio's way. Otherwise they were out of the financing. We'd simply close on a lesser amount. Interest rates had eased quite a bit since they were initially set and our proposal was very attractive. During this time, the Pru demonstrated their mettle by backing up the position we were taking when these prospective lenders complained to them about the high-handed tactics that were being employed. Within three days, all of the reluctant participants in the private placement had acquiesced. The first closing was scheduled for 11 a.m. on November 13, 1975.

Sohio's proceeds from the first closing were $716 million. We had $780 million of commercial paper outstanding, and we used part of the proceeds to reduce that amount by $440 million. We paid down $175 million of our bank loans. Subsequent closings took place over the next year or so to complete the $1.75 billion offering.

Having successfully completed the largest private placement ever, we were confident that we had broken the back of our financial challenge and had put to rest, once and for all, concerns about our ability to finance our Alaskan project.

Little did we know.

A blizzard of paperwork at the first closing of the $1.75 billion private placement by Sohio/BP Trans Alaska Pipeline Capital. This financing was by far the largest US private placement in history and was followed by another private placement of $500 million, which also ranked among the largest such financings.

MORGAN STANLEY & CO.
Incorporated
1251 Avenue of the Americas
New York, N.Y. 10020

December 17, 1975

RECEIVED

DEC 2 9 1975

J. R. MILLER

Mr. John R. Miller
Vice President - Finance
The Standard Oil Company
Midland Building
Cleveland, Ohio 44115

Dear John:

Lots of special things seemed to be involved with the pipeline financing yesterday. Along with some of the other things that happened, the mementos that we ordered came in and I am enclosing one for you herewith.

I think you know how I feel about you as a business man and that I have the highest regard for you and all your associates in this respect. I do want to say in writing, however, how much I appreciated your sense of humor and your patience no matter how sorely tried and no matter how many times you gave me speeches one through ten. I really believe that without your calming influence we might have all fallen apart in the course of that long hot summer, spring and fall. You did a fantastic job and I hope that your seniors appreciate it.

I am looking forward to working on the next of your financing programs with you and I hope we will be under a little less pressure on future endeavors.

Say Merry Christmas to Karen and have one yourself.

Very truly yours,

David P. Goodman
Managing Director

29. WINDOW DRESSING

David Goodman was constantly on the lookout for unique pockets of money for Sohio, recognizing that we needed to tap as many sources of funds as possible to meet our demands. In the spring of 1976, Morgan Stanley began hearing that investors outside of major financial centers had fewer opportunities to invest short term at interest rates that were as attractive as those available to their counterparts in places like New York, Chicago, and San Francisco. During one of the ad hoc brainstorming sessions of our core finance team—myself, David Goodman, George Dunn, Sam Pryor, and Bob Lovejoy—to figure out what to do next, David threw out the idea of a public offering of short-term notes, something that had never been done before. Investment instruments with short maturities typically took the form of bank offerings such as certificates of deposit, and the like.

In the course of raising a lot of money, the finance team had already used a number of novel, innovative, and unconventional approaches, to the point that now, when we came up with something that "had never been done before," we automatically concluded that's what we should do!

Having thus determined the general form of the next financing, we began working out the specifics. We settled on a three-part offering: $150 million, $50 million and $75 million of notes maturing in 18 months, three years, and five years, respectively. The proceeds of the three- and five-year notes would pay the Alaskan crude oil reserves tax due in June 1976. The 18-month notes would provide interim financing to offset expenditures for the development of our North Slope properties and the construction of TAPS.

If things went according to plan, the registration statement would become effective before the middle of March. Selling the notes would commence, and as was always the case, delivery of the notes would take place exactly two weeks later, or before the end of the month. The maturity date of the notes would be based on the date of closing, that is, eighteen months, three years, or five years from the date of delivery.

Whenever we began working on a specific financing, I would update the financial plan, taking into account the proposed transaction. As part of this exercise, I would calculate a number of pro forma financial ratios, such as debt-to-equity, coverage of fixed charges, etc. As I did so for this particular offering, it became apparent that, because the eighteen-month notes would mature shortly before the end of September of 1977, they would move from long-term debt to a short-term liability, that is debt due to be paid within the next twelve months, on our balance sheet to be published at the end of the third quarter of 1976. If, however, we delayed the delivery of the notes to April 1, then the maturity date for the eighteen-month notes would be October 1, 1977, and therefore wouldn't show up as a current liability until we published our 1976 annual report sometime in February of 1977. But, under GAAP, if we could show that we had put in place long-term borrowing arrangements to replace the 18-month notes, and further, that it was our intention to do that, we could continue to book the short-term notes as long-term debt.

Why was this a significant issue? An additional $150 million of current liabilities would wreak havoc with our liquidity ratios, something that a number of buyers of our commercial paper paid close attention to, as did the rating agencies, and most likely, owners and prospective buyers of our long-term debt. Although these measures—current ratio and quick ratio—are used to assess the ability of a company to satisfy its current liabilities and to protect its short-term creditors, long-term creditors obviously become concerned, as well, if there is reason to believe that a company may not survive in the short run.

This was an important issue, and there were a couple of ways to resolve it favorably. We could delay the offering about a week, but that ran the risk of a favorable market turning against us. Or we could sell the notes as scheduled but delay their delivery about a week longer than was traditional. I called David to see if that would create a problem. Upon reflection, he indicated it was doable, and so we moved the maturity dates to October 1 for the eighteen-month notes and to April 1 for the three- and five-year notes.

While there are those who, for good reason, look with disfavor upon using gimmickry to dress up financial statements, in our case, we were simply giving ourselves a little extra time to put long-term arrangements in place to be able to book the liabilities in question as long-term ones. That result would avoid a situation where the information might otherwise be misinterpreted by those looking strictly at certain ratios, without a good understanding of the overall picture, and perhaps, drawing a wrong conclusion to our detriment.

It was a justifiable approach in my opinion.

Maybe I was too clever by half, as the British would say. In the midst of getting organized to proceed with the offering, I was unexpectedly summoned to a meeting of the management committee, a small group of Sohio's top executives—Charlie Spahr, Sohio's chairman; Al Whitehouse, president; Joe Harnett, executive vice president; Don Stevens, senior vice president; and my boss, Paul Phillips—who gathered every Monday morning. The committee had been discussing our financial situation and questioning what we were planning to do next. Paul suggested bringing me into the meeting to talk about it. I explained that I was in the early stages of working out the details, that I hadn't had an opportunity to review the ideas for the next offering with Paul, but that I had hoped to be in a position to bring it to the board of directors for approval at the next regularly scheduled meeting.

I then proceeded to lay out the specifics of what I was proposing to do. I also made note of the extension of the delivery date and the favorable accounting treatment that would result. Paul reacted negatively to the idea, and I found myself having to defend my proposal from my boss's attacks. Not a good situation. Blood was in the water. And as I had witnessed on previous occasions, when that happens, it becomes sport for the members of the management committee, and they all, with the exception of Charlie Spahr, started piling on.

Under normal circumstances, I would know in advance that I was expected to make an appearance before the management committee and would have taken time to prepare a presentation, including visual aids, designed to convey an understanding of the matter under review. In this case, I was left to giving a verbal explanation of some rather arcane accounting issues and was struggling in vain to make my point. Finally, after about an hour of getting nowhere, Charlie Spahr ended the discussion. He instructed me to call General Shepard, chairman of the Financial Advisory Committee, to schedule a review of my proposal before the next board meeting. He further instructed me to tell General Shepard that some of the members of the management committee disagreed with the idea, but he and I thought it was the right thing to do. Charlie's brief summation—with no reference to financial or accounting issues—immediately cleared up the confusion. Almost in unison, everyone voiced their support of my idea, saying their questions and concerns had been addressed to their satisfaction.

The proposed offering survived Sohio's approval process and we proceeded with it.

30. DIVINE INTERVENTION

There is an extensive amount of printing involved in offering securities to the public. Prior to our first public offering after our amalgamation with BP, one of the issues that needed to be resolved was where we were going to do the printing.

Because it would be more convenient for them, Morgan Stanley wanted to print in New York. However, the cost of printing in Cleveland was significantly less, and for that reason, our preference was to use a local printer, Judson Brooks, whose operations were located just a few blocks from our headquarters.

We reached a workable compromise once Morgan Stanley was satisfied Judson Brooks was up to the job. That is to say, they had the expertise to produce documents that met the SEC's rigorous requirements, Ronaldson Slope type—Morgan Stanley's font of choice, and ample supplies of "Morgan Stanley blue" ink. The registration statements would be printed in Cleveland, but the underwriting agreements, part of the package of information filed with the Securities and Exchange Commission, would be printed in New York to make it easier to get those documents signed.

The offering process starts with a preliminary prospectus, or "red herring," so called for the legend in red type that appeared in the margin of the cover page cautioning readers that although a registration statement relating to these securities had been filed with the SEC, the securities may not be sold until the commission issues an order stating that the registration statement had become effective. The price at which the securities are to be offered—interest rates in the case of debt securities and per-share prices in the case of stock—is left blank on the cover of the preliminary prospectus, although an estimate of the maximum dollar amount of the offering is provided in the registration statement for purposes of determining the SEC's registration fee. That fee must be paid either by certified check or cash at the time of the initial filing. Once filed, the underwriters widely distribute the red herring to prospective investors to acquaint them with the merchandise that is going to be offered for sale.

For the "triple header" offering of $325 million of notes in March 1976, about 12,500 preliminary prospectuses were distributed. A short time later, we filed the first amendment to the registration statement, addressing comments or questions raised by the SEC examiner assigned to the offering. The SEC was satisfied with our response, and we asked them to issue the order that the registration statement become effective on March 11.

On the day before, after the financial markets closed, we negotiated the interest rates to be paid on the notes with Morgan Stanley, the lead underwriter. Demand for the eighteen month notes was high, so we increased the amount of those notes to be offered by $50 million. That increase would raise the SEC registration fee by $10 thousand more than was paid with the initial filing, and the incremental fee would be due when we filed the package in the morning. A banker was standing by to cut a certified check, should one be needed.

Along with the finance team, I headed off for the usual long night at the printers to update the prospectus by removing the red herring legend, filling in the blank spots with the interest rates on the notes, putting in other information relating to the pricing of the securities, and changing the color of the print from black to Morgan Stanley blue. These changes were given to the printer, who soon reappeared with galleys to be proofread and verified. We made minor fixes until the prospectus was in apple pie order. Mass printing of the final prospectuses began, and the filing package, sans the underwriting documents, was packaged to be flown to Washington, DC, first thing in the morning. A lawyer coming from

New York with the underwriting documents would meet the flight, merge the separate components of the filing package, and then file them with the SEC when it opened for business.

While we were waiting for copies of the final prospectus to come off the printing press, George Dunn, who had completed his work for the night, told me he was flying to Washington early the next morning to attend a meeting and volunteered to take along our portion of the filing package. Having the messenger hand the package off to George at the airport in the morning seemed like a sensible alternative to sending the messenger to Washington. George would take the package on his flight to DC and then give it to the New York lawyer who would be at the gate awaiting his arrival. Arrangements were made, and George left for home. The rest of us stayed around to box up the final prospectuses, the certified check, and other sundry documents needed for the filing package.

My work done, I left for home to get a few hours' sleep.

Rising early the next morning, George caught the rapid transit to Cleveland Hopkins Airport. Overnight, there had been a wicked "lake-effect" snowstorm, and the rapid got stuck in the snow and derailed. Realizing he wasn't going to make it to Hopkins, George got out and tromped through the snow to the next station where there was a pay phone. (Remember, no cell phones in those days.) He called Judson Brooks, explained his dilemma and asked the printer to instruct the messenger to deliver the package to Bob Johnson, an attorney who worked for George and who was also flying to Washington that morning to attend the same meeting George had planned to attend. George then made his way back to the office.

Despite the late nights at the printer, I always got to the office early the next morning to wait for the call confirming the package had been filed, and the SEC had declared the registration statement effective. Then I would monitor the sales effort through the course of the day. Shortly after I arrived at the office that particular morning, my phone rang. It wasn't the confirmation call I was expecting. It was George calling to say we didn't get filed.

"Are you serious?" I asked.

"Yes," he said, explaining that he had missed his flight. Bob Johnson had called when he got to Washington, asking whether he should go ahead with the meeting without George. "Yes," George had said. "And by the way, did you deliver the filing package?" Bob had no idea what George was talking about. He never received the package from the messenger at Hopkins Airport.

Having told me this, George hung up. In a state of near panic, I began running down the things I would need to get to the SEC pronto: one signed and two conformed copies of the registration statement and three sets of the exhibits; eight additional conformed copies of the registration statement, five of which were marked to indicate the changes from Amendment No. 1; eight copies of the Agreement Among Underwriters with the form of Underwriting Agreement attached; eight copies of the forms of indentures; and a certified check, or cash, in the amount of $10,000 to pay the incremental SEC registration fees. A daunting task, but one with a lot riding on it. I would also need transportation to Washington, so I picked up the phone and called the individual responsible for Sohio's aircraft, explained that I had an emergency situation, and told him that if we had one of our planes at Hopkins, not to let it leave until he heard from me.

I was about to call Judson Brooks to pull together some of the documents when my phone rang: it was George telling me we were filed.

George and I spent the next few hours trying to deconstruct the events that had led to a successful filing at the SEC, seemingly untouched by human hands. We tracked down the Judson Brooks messenger, who assured us he had faithfully followed our instructions. When he arrived with the package at Hopkins Airport, he asked the information desk to page a Mr. Johnson, who was a passenger on flight so and so going to Washington, DC. A gentleman approached the desk and identified himself as Mr. Johnson. The messenger gave him the package and told him someone would meet him at the gate when he arrived in Washington and he was to turn the package over to him. Mr. Johnson said OK and headed for the plane, package in hand. (Try that today with the TSA.)

About that same time, attorney Ken Lippman was boarding a New York train heading for Washington with the underwriting agreements. Ken was supposed to meet the flight from Cleveland, retrieve the Judson Brooks' package, merge it with the underwriting documents, and proceed to the SEC to file the offering. George and I caught up with Ken later in the morning. He told us he had met the Cleveland flight and scanned the disembarking passengers but had recognized no one. No one appeared to be looking for him, either. Finally, all of the passengers had gotten off the plane and were headed for the exits. Ken was about to give up when a stewardess walked off the plane with a package in her hand. Ken, who had conducted this assignment on previous occasions, noticed the package was secured with Judson's Brooks' signature green and white tape. He told the stewardess the package was his. Ken had not been a passenger on the plane, so the stewardess was skeptical of his claim. After more discussion, she called for her supervisor. Ken explained who he was and told the supervisor what was in the package. The supervisor opened it, and sure enough, the contents were exactly as Ken had described, so he was allowed to take the package and leave. Shortly thereafter, he filed the documents with the SEC. Mission accomplished.

We'll never know for sure what happened, but the only thing that George and I could conclude was the wrong Mr. Johnson took the package on the plane with him, had second thoughts about what the hell he was doing, and left the package on the plane.

Later that afternoon, George and I were waiting in Sohio's boardroom for a meeting with senior management to start. We were laughing about our good fortune when Charlie Spahr asked what was so funny. Office politics were minimal at Sohio, which was a good thing because politics was not my forte. That said, I was shrewd enough to know, "It's none of your business," was a bad response. Trapped, I briefly told the story, suggesting we were the fortunate recipients of divine intervention.

Unfortunately, Charlie failed to see the humor in all of this. Although he was a God-fearing Baptist, he made it clear that he preferred to rely on sound practices and procedures rather than help from above to get the job done.

Fortunately, demand for the notes was strong, and the offering went smoothly, with $200 million of the notes maturing in eighteen months, the shortest maturity ever for a public offering. All told, we raised $325 million at attractive rates: the 18-month, three-year and five-year notes carried interest rates of 7.1 percent, 7.6 percent, and 8 percent, respectively.

The market remained attractive, so we decided to tap it again. On April 27th, Sohio Pipe Line Company issued $250 million of twenty five-year debentures to the public. But this time, heeding Charlie's edict, we filed in a conventional manner.

31. PRIVATE PLACEMENT MULLIGAN

The federal right-of-way permit mandated that we X-ray 100 percent of the welds connecting the sections of pipe which came in lengths of forty-to-sixty feet. Typically, only 10 percent would be X-rayed as a means of controlling the quality of the welds, but because of extremely restrictive environmental standards, we were required to X-ray each and every one. X-ray crews strapped a twelve-foot strip of X-ray film around each weld, then shot the X-ray. In areas where the pipeline was to be buried, and was, therefore, resting on the bottom of the ditch, a "bell hole" had to be excavated around the weld in order to accommodate the X-ray equipment, a time-consuming process. It was highly desirable for the X-ray crews to stay close behind the welding crews, so if any flaws were detected, the welding crews could be notified and corrections made to their procedures before too many bad welds were made. That would enable the crews backfilling the ditches to keep pace as well.

Alyeska had contracted with two companies to do the X-ray work. Ketchbaw Industries had the contract for X-raying the welds south of the Yukon River. During the 1975 construction season, Ketchbaw had difficulty keeping up with the welding crews. A lot of pressure was put on them to catch up, which they did. Turns out, they would set up their equipment to take an X-ray of a weld, snap several X-rays of the same weld, and then leapfrog down the line, skipping several welds in the process. While that enabled them to get caught up, it was clearly in violation of the permit stipulations.

All of this came to light in September of 1975 when a former employee of Ketchbaw, Peter Kelley, sued the company, claiming he had been fired because he had refused to participate in falsifying the X-rays. A soap opera ensued: a manager who had worked for Ketchbaw died of cyanide poisoning, and welding X-rays turned up missing from one of the construction camps, presumably stolen.

To determine the extent of the problem, Alyeska began a review of the 30,800 welds that had been made in 1975 and found that 3,955 of them were questionable. About 10 percent of the welding problems that were identified were too minor to be of concern, but the rest would have to be examined again and repaired, if necessary. That meant digging up the welds in cases where the pipeline had been buried.

Alyeska reported its findings to the Interior Department in the spring of 1976. In July, Congress held hearings on the matter, and President Gerald Ford sent a team to Alaska to oversee Alyeska's work. In the meantime, Alyeska began inspecting the questionable welds. By September, more than 3,000 of them had either been redone or certified as safe, and by the end of November, waivers were asked for the thirty-four welds remaining to be examined. Of these, President Ford's team would grant waivers for only three welds that were buried seventeen feet under the Koyukuk River, insisting that the other thirty-one be dug up and repaired.

Alyeska estimated the cost of this entire debacle to be about $55 million.

III

In January 1976, Alyeska announced that the new estimate to complete construction of TAPS was $7 billion, an increase of $600 million over the estimate produced in May of the previous year. On June 30th, Alyeska increased its cost estimate to $7.7 billion. It was now evident that we would not comply with the restrictions imposed by the "project allowable" covenant in our private placement agreement, which limited the amount of indebtedness that we could incur for our Alaskan venture to $3.75 billion.

I set up a meeting with Ray Charles, senior vice president at Prudential, and head of its Bond and Commercial Loan Department, to discuss our situation and to update him on the X-ray saga. He put forth the idea of going back to our private placement participants to ask them for relief on the project allowable covenant and to participate in a second Sohio/BP Trans Alaska Pipeline Capital financing. By putting up more money, they would enhance our chances of being able to secure the funds we needed to complete our Alaskan project, thereby protecting their original investments.

On July 20th Morgan Stanley circulated a mark-up of the original private placement offering memorandum to those who had participated in that transaction. The revised memorandum set forth the proposed changes to the original covenants and offered investors an opportunity to purchase 9¾ percent notes of Capital, due either in 1993 or 1998, contingent upon receiving the covenant modifications. The amount of the offering was $300 million, but we indicated a willingness to increase it to $500 million.

The offering went smoothly, and on September 15th, we closed. Total amount of the offering was $500 million, of which $339 million would be for Sohio Pipe Line Company's account. And the project allowable covenant was modified to allow us to incur up to $5 billion to finance expenditures for the production and transportation of Prudhoe Bay oil.

32. COLD CALL REDUX

lmost a year had passed since I last saw or heard from Duke Johnson of Nova Scotia Bank when he made that fortuitous cold call on Sohio in the autumn of 1975. This time, he called to make an appointment. I happily accommodated him, thinking there was a good chance we could increase the amount of our revolving credit with his bank from $100 million to $200 million.

Duke arrived with an assistant, Paul Schultz, which I interpreted as a rise in status for Duke. They sat on the couch in front of the desk in my small, dingy office. I had heard the Bank of Nova Scotia held a contest the previous year and that Duke had won by bringing the most new business into the bank by virtue of Sohio's $100 million revolving credit. The prize had been a week's vacation in the Caribbean for Duke and his family .

After the usual brief exchange of pleasantries—I wasn't good at small talk—I turned to Duke and asked, "How would you like to win a trip around the world?"

Paul nearly fell off the couch, laughing. When he regained his composure, he explained that on the flight from Toronto, Duke had told Paul he suspected I would ask to increase our line to $200 million, which would put Duke in good shape for this year's contest. That incentive, and perhaps more important, the good relationship we had developed with the bank, earned us quick approval of the increase.

I never heard how Duke fared in that year's contest. But on numerous occasions, I told my counterparts in Cleveland's business community—a goodly number of Fortune 500 companies, in those days—what a genuine pleasure it was working with Duke, and they should get to know him and consider doing business with the Bank of Nova Scotia. Over time, the bank booked enough new business that it opened an office in Cleveland.

Duke was picked to run it.

III

As the bad news piled up, we made it a point to communicate regularly with the rating agencies, along with all of our major creditors, keeping them informed of developments and educating them on their impacts on Sohio. We got high marks for our candor, our integrity, and our forward planning. With the exception of rising crude oil prices, almost all the news was unfavorable, making it important to deal with it in a timely, forthright, and proactive manner. The most damaging news was the endless stream of higher cost estimates. To deal with this, we updated our financial forecast to demonstrate that the economics of the project remained favorable by dint of higher crude oil prices, which fortunately kept fairly close pace with the project's escalating cost. In fact, it could be argued the two bore some relationship, one with the other. An illustration that we began to deploy to allay concerns over cost increases was the "break-even" landed price of crude oil, that is, the price of Prudhoe Bay crude delivered to California that would be necessary to keep the project's economics above water. This concept, conceived by David Goodman, was designed to give the reviewer comfort that the project remained economically viable. Thankfully, despite the higher costs we were experiencing the break-even price was always higher than what crude was actually selling for. Furthermore, a fair amount of cushion always existed.

III

At the end of September, in an effort to keep pace with our expenditures in Alaska, which during 1976 would total $1.7 billion, or close to $200,000 an hour, we entered into a $500 million revolving credit and term loan agreement with a group of banks. Then we began thinking about squeezing off another public offering of notes before year-end. 1976 was a presidential election year, and there was considerable concern on Wall Street over the money markets' reaction if Jimmy Carter were to oust President Ford. Potential issuers were being advised to delay financings until the election was over, and if Carter won, until the market for debt securities became favorable again.

I was a contrarian on this prevailing view. I believed, as was true with most market moving macro events, if Carter won, the markets would probably overreact, go into convulsions, and then, fairly quickly, return to some semblance of normality. So going against conventional wisdom, we made preparations to proceed with an offering of another $350 million of Sohio notes. If my premise proved wrong, we could always pull the deal. It was not. When investors began to look for buying opportunities after the election, we were the only ones in the marketplace. Everyone else had heeded the advice that they should defer. On December 2nd, we sold $75 million of notes due in three years, $75 million due in five years, and $200 million due in ten years at attractive interest rates: 6⅛ percent, 6½ percent and 7½ percent for the three-year, five-year, and ten-year notes, respectively. The proceeds from the three- and five-year notes were used to fund the 1977 installment of the Alaska tax on Prudhoe Bay reserves.

Sohio's finance team accomplished a good deal in 1976. Running what we began referring to as the Bond of the Month Club, we secured $1.3 billion of permanent financing, plus an additional $600 million of bank credit for our Alaskan venture. By now, we had raised $4.3 billion of the estimated $5.2 billion of external financing we would need to complete the development of the Prudhoe Bay field and related transportation projects. Although much remained to be done, the end was clearly in sight with construction on schedule for a startup of TAPS in the third quarter of the coming year.

III

With the happy prospect that, at long last, our Alaskan venture would start yielding a return rather than representing a black hole sucking up every dollar we could get our hands on, my financial forecasts for 1977 began to look a little rosier, reflecting an influx of cash by the end of the year. Looking beyond that year of transition, there was absolutely no doubt that Sohio was going to become a much different company.

That realization got me thinking about the broader implications of what was on the horizon. We had spent the last seven years pinching pennies and nursing nickels, and now we were about to generate gargantuan amounts of cash. As an economy move, the organization had gotten a lot thinner since the inception of our Alaskan ordeal. The Corporate Planning Department had been disbanded. Although in years past we had trained a lot of people to evaluate capital expenditure prospects, many of them had moved on or retired and had not been replaced. All this led me to believe that it was not too early to begin making preparations for what was coming, and reinstituting the planning department seemed to me to be a good place to start.

I began to discuss my concerns with Paul, prodding him to convince senior management of the need to take steps to deal with a much different set of circumstances. Finally, most likely to get me off his back, Paul asked me to write a white paper on the rationale for and the benefits of reestablishing a planning department. With that in hand, he would bring it up with Charlie Spahr.

I put together what I thought was a convincing argument for my case. One of the points that I made was a comparison of certain attributes of oil companies that were of a size that we were about to become. One in particular was the number of employees they had, typically a factor of two or more times, relative to our staffing levels. While I readily acknowledged that this comparison could be challenged as rather meaningless, I felt it served as a good proxy to illustrate the magnitude of the change we were going to experience. Paul, good to his word, discussed my white paper with Charlie, and as a result, the decision was made to add planning to my responsibilities. My title was changed from vice president, finance, to vice president, finance and planning. Of course, due to the need to continue our frugal ways in the immediate future, I wasn't permitted to add anyone to my staff.

As these things go, somehow the organization got wind of my comparison of employee levels, and the buzz around the office was that I had recommended hiring 75,000 people. Sometimes in the hallways and water cooler conversations, the subtler point gets lost.

33. ROUNDING THIRD AND HEADING FOR HOME

Although 1976 was a banner year for finance, much remained to be done in 1977, the final year of construction of TAPS. On March 15th, we issued $250 million of Standard Oil thirty-year debentures in a public offering, the proceeds of which were to be used to meet expenditures for the development of Sohio's interests on the North Slope and related transportation facilities.

Next, we turned our attention to finding a way to finance the six new tankers to be used to ship oil from the Port of Valdez to the Lower 48. Under the Merchant Marine Act of 1920 (the Jones Act), these tankers had to be built and registered in the United States, owned, and operated by US citizens, and manned by US crews. In order for a company to qualify as a "US citizen" under the Jones Act, foreign ownership could not exceed twenty-five percent. Given BP's ownership in Sohio, we didn't meet the requirement for US citizenship. Therefore, we couldn't own outright the six tankers that we had under construction and we had to resort to a convoluted leveraged lease and charter arrangement to finance them.

To comply with the Jones Act, we assigned the construction contracts for the six tankers to entities such as General Motors Acceptance Corporation, GE Credit Corporation, and commercial banks, all of which were US citizens. Under a leveraged lease arrangement, these companies provided the equity portion, or 30 percent, of the construction costs, leaving 70 percent of the costs to be financed by the issuance of debt. One of the positive features of the Jones Act was a provision, Title XI, that allowed the US Department of Commerce Maritime Administration to guarantee indebtedness to be incurred for ship construction. Taking advantage of this provision to lower our interest costs, we made arrangements for the US government to guarantee all of the debt.

To secure the debt portion of the leveraged leases for two of the tankers, we privately placed $109 million of bonds. Debt for the remaining four tankers was secured through a $248 million public offering later in the year, the largest ever offering of Title XI bonds. As the final step in each of these six transactions, upon delivery of the vessels, the owners would enter into a time charter arrangement to Sohio.

III

Another opportunity to secure low cost funding for our Alaskan venture came in the form of industrial revenue bonds, a fairly common financing technique. Such bonds are issued by states or political subdivisions of states for the purpose of building and equipping facilities that are then leased to private enterprise. Sometimes, but not always, the interest on such bonds are exempt from federal income tax, and buyers of tax exempt bonds are willing to accept a lower interest rate. In those cases, it's a win-win situation. The issuer gains employment and property tax revenues while the company benefits from the reduced cost of financing the facilities to be leased.

Although the Internal Revenue Code provides that interest on such obligations for industrial development projects are not exempt from federal income taxes, there is an exception when the proceeds from such bond offerings are used to provide docks, wharves, and facilities directly related thereto.

Bingo.

The cost to Sohio and BP for their undivided interests in the TAPS Marine Terminal at Valdez worked out to be approximately $665 million and, working with the City of Valdez, an arrangement was entered into whereby they would issue revenue bonds in that amount for the purpose of acquiring a leasehold interest in the terminal from Sohio Pipe Line and BP Pipelines. The City of Valdez would then sublease their interest back to the pipe line companies. Consistent with past joint financings, Sohio's share would be 67.8 percent, and BP's would be 32.2 percent.

Because of the magnitude of the financing, Morgan Stanley recommended breaking it up into two pieces. The first offering of $350 million of the City of Valdez, Alaska Series A Marine Terminal Bonds, the largest industrial revenue bond offering ever, was sold to the public on June 30th with the closing scheduled for July 14th. The second offering of $315 million of Series B bonds was sold on August 24th.

III

Murphy's Law, which had plagued us from the very beginning, proved its authenticity by raising its ugly head twice in the course of the first industrial revenue bond offering, and once again in between the two.

By mid-year, the pipeline was ready for startup, which is a tricky procedure. On June 20, 1977, oil was introduced into the line. Initially, the throughput rate was very low to allow the operators to closely monitor the system for leaks or other problems that might arise, and to let the hot oil and the cold pipeline reach thermal equilibrium as it slowly made its way to Valdez. Although a number of difficulties were encountered, the startup proceeded rather smoothly until, on July 8th, the oil reached Pump Station Number 8, which was located approximately 490 miles south of Prudhoe Bay. Workers there were replacing a strainer on one of the pumps, when, through operator error, oil sprayed from the open strainer into the pump house causing an explosion and fire that killed one worker, and essentially destroyed the building and the pump equipment. Subsequently, the station was bypassed, and the first barrel of oil finally reached the Valdez terminal by the end of July.

The first revenue bond offering had been sold when the explosion occurred, but the closing had yet to take place.

With the uncertainty the explosion introduced, it was necessary to circulate to the buyers of the bonds a supplement to the prospectus, informing them of the accident and its repercussions. Repairing Pump Station Number 8 would take six-to-eight months. Commercial operation of TAPS was still estimated to commence in the third quarter of 1977, but the initial design capacity of 1.2 million barrels per day could not be attained. Maximum throughput until the damaged station was recommissioned was estimated to be about 800,000 barrels per day.

Fortunately, none of the investors backed out.

Then, as the Ides of July approached, my home phone rang during the wee hours of the morning. It was Ron McGimpsey. He was in New York preparing for the revenue bond closing, which was to take place later that morning. From the noise in the background, I could tell Ron was in a bar. He said he was calling to let me know there were two problems. First, the bar was running out of ice and second, we were not going to close.

The second issue Ron raised got my undivided attention. He recounted the events of his day. Late in the afternoon as the team was preparing to go through its pre-closing routine at the offices of the Morgan Guaranty Trust, the lights went out. After waiting awhile for the lights to come back on, the team decided to leave, taking the stairs down a goodly number of floors because the elevators were not working. The streets of New York were pitch black. The team members managed to find their way to a bar that was lit by candles. As time went by—and with the power still off—they concluded there was no way to close the deal in the morning. Our best-laid plans were blown astray by what later would be known as the great New York Blackout.

When Bala Ganesan, my commercial paper manager par excellence, arrived at the office the next morning, I was standing in his doorway to greet him with the news of the blackout and subsequent failure to close on our financing. I told him this was a golden opportunity to test the contingency plan I required him to develop every time we anticipated receiving funds from a closing, just in case we didn't.

Off he went.

A couple of hours later, Bala popped into my office with a big smile on his face. In putting his plan together—what credit agreements he could draw down on by virtue of pre-arranged waivers of the notice requirements in emergency situations such as this, what discretionary expenditures could be delayed, etc.—he figured he needed to come up with something close to the amount of commercial paper that had been stacked up in expectation that the closing would occur and needed to be repaid.

Although power had been restored in the suburbs that morning, the City of New York itself was still blacked out, and financial markets in the city were closed. Consequently, holders of our commercial paper couldn't present our IOUs for payment, so Bala needed only to cover the paper that had been sold in Chicago, or about twenty-five percent of the total amount maturing that day, leaving him with excess cash available. Under the circumstances, short-term money rates had spiked because of New York's shut down, allowing him to put the excess cash to work overnight, making a nice return for a day's work. In addition to a good outcome, Bala—who was annoyed at my insistence over the years on planning for contingencies such as this, to no avail—was now converted to a true believer in its virtue.

III

On August 4th, as we were preparing the documents for the Series B offering of Marine Terminal Bonds, Alyeska delivered to the owners of TAPS a budget reflecting a capital cost for TAPS of $8 billion, including the costs associated with the final testing of the system and preparation for commercial operations. These cost estimates did not include interest during construction. Taken interest into account, approximately $400 million during construction, Sohio's share of the cost of TAPS was now estimated to be $3.1 billion, bringing the estimate of total expenditures for our Alaskan venture to $6.3 billion.

But Murphy be damned, once we completed the Series B offering, although we still had to finance the proposed pipeline from Long Beach, California to Midland, Texas, financing of the development of the Prudhoe Bay oil field, the Trans Alaska Pipeline, and the Valdez terminal was done.

It was about this time that the business press began to write stories about the project. Two themes were predominate. First was recognition that the financing was of epic proportion relative to Sohio's size at the outset and, despite the belief held by many knowledgeable people that it couldn't be done, we had succeeded. Second was the transformation that this project would have on Sohio, from a Midwestern refiner and marketer of crude oil to a fully integrated petroleum company and one of the two largest holders of domestic crude oil reserves.

In the interviews that took place, the issue of how our Alaskan venture, which was originally estimated to cost us $500 million, could have ended up costing us over $6 billion, almost always came up. Whenever that question was put to Paul, he would begin his answer with, "Well, you need to understand, the first estimate was a bad one."

And every time, I would mutter under my breath, "No, kidding, Paul."

Or words to that effect.

34. SUMMARY OF FINANCIAL ACCOMPLISHMENTS

The total cost of Sohio's involvement in its Alaskan project, excluding PacTex, which never came to fruition, but including $400 million of interest during construction, was $5.9 billion. Contrast that to the company's total assets of $773 million at the onset of the project. During the three peak TAPS construction years—1975, 1976, and 1977—Sohio's average requirement for external sources of funds exceeded $100 million every single month. Most of the funds Sohio raised to finance the project and plug the holes in cash flow were in the form of debt.

To accomplish this, the transactions we crafted over the eight-year period from early 1970 through the end of 1977 were often intricate and unconventional—the result of highly creative thinking by our finance team. A number of these transactions represented first-ever or largest-ever, at the time. The private placement of $1.75 billion by Sohio/BP Trans Alaska Pipeline Capital was by far the largest ever US private placement in history and was followed by another private placement of $500 million, which also ranked among the largest such financings. The $350 million offering of Series A Valdez Marine Terminal bonds, followed by a similar $315 million offering, was the largest ever industrial revenue bond offering. The bonds issued to finance a portion of the cost of building our Jones Act tankers was the largest offering of Title XI debt ever. And our issue of 18-month notes was the first-ever public offering of notes of such short duration.

In addition to permanent financing, during the four-year period from 1974 to 1977, Sohio issued a total of $13.7 billion of commercial paper, and at one point, had $780 million of paper outstanding, which represented about seven percent of the non-financial, dealer-placed paper market.

A summary of Sohio's sources of external funds for our Alaskan project is set forth below:

SOURCES OF FUNDS (dollars in millions)

Sohio Pipe Line Debt	
Bank Debt	$ 600
Public Offerings	589
Private Placements	1,526
Valdez Revenue Bonds	451
Leveraged Lease of Equipment	62
Standard Oil Debt	
Bank Debt	900
Alaskan Tax Financings	275
Other Public Offerings	800
Advanced Sales of Crude Oil	475
Tanker Financings	
Equity	153
Title XI Debt	357
Standard Oil Sale of Equity	137
Total External Financings	$ 6,325

Aside from the Hospitality Motor Inns initial public offering that enabled it to finance future growth on its own, in our spare time we arranged $300 million of financings for other parts of our business. Those transactions included a $100 million public offering of debentures for general corporate purposes, $125 million of production payment financings for the development of new coal mines, $60 million of Environmental Improvement Revenue bonds for air and water quality control facilities for our refineries and a

$15 million production payment loan to develop our uranium mine.

In August of 1977, *Fortune* wrote that "seldom in the business of raising money have so few, who knew so little, done so much." I'll grant the author "few" and "much," but it's hard to imagine what more we could have accomplished, even if we had known what we were doing.

35. THE AFTERMATH

1 978, the first full year of Alaskan operations, ushered in a new era for Sohio. Although capital requirements for our Alaskan venture remained high, for the first time since 1972, our cash flow from operations was sufficient to cover our capital expenditures of $762 million.

On a final visit to the rating agencies—a courtesy call since our Alaskan project was essentially complete and it was obvious that our venture was an overwhelming success—I ran into an unexpected reception at S&P. I was by myself, and with our money-raising days rapidly ending, I hadn't prepared a formal presentation. My purpose was to express my appreciation for both agencies' support over the years. But the staff at S&P had a presentation of their own that they wanted to share with me.

Russ Fraser—the key if not sole supporter of Sohio at S&P—had recently left the agency to join Paine Webber. We had heard that Russ's staff took issue with his initial rating, arguing that a downgrade would be more appropriate. We further heard that Russ held his ground, countering that he had even contemplated upgrading us to "AAA." Fortunately for him, he didn't. As time went by, with the onset of project delays and skyrocketing costs, the debate between Russ and his staff intensified. But Russ hung in there with us, his only concession being a slight downgrade to AA minus as the bad news accumulated.

Now unbridled by the departure of Russ, his former staff members let me know what they thought. They showed me a schedule composed of information culled from numerous presentations we had made over the years. For each presentation, our estimates of total expenditures for our Alaskan venture and when we expected to startup TAPS were laid out. Final costs were more than ten times higher than we had originally thought, and startup was five-to-six years later. I can only surmise they wanted to humiliate me with evidence that my ability to divine the future was grossly deficient. Perhaps they were looking for an apology, but the best I could muster was, "Picky, picky."

I found it amusing, and I broke out laughing. "Why now?" I asked. "It's over." I assured them our creditors would be repaid in full and on schedule. Moreover, the Sohio paper they held was now a better security than S&P's rating indicated. So they, or at least Russ, could take comfort in the fact that they didn't have disgruntled investors on their hands, which I attributed to keeping S&P apprised of our situation every step of the way. I was tempted to suggest they seek counsel from Mr. Esokait at Moody's, but I thought better of it.

Declaring victory on the financial front, my job of raising money was over, and early in 1978, I was reassigned as vice president of transportation, responsible for Sohio's pipelines and our new fleet of ships. My major challenge was to build an organization to manage our marine operations, which was no small task. Fortunately, BP had decades of experience transporting oil by tankers, and calling upon their expertise, together, we put in place a first-class Marine Department.

In December of 1979, I was elected senior vice president, technology, and chemicals, and became a member of the management committee. My portfolio of responsibilities also included engineering, and research and development. Although I had barely begun to get my arms around my new assignment, some eight months later, on the 1st of August of 1980, much to my surprise, I was elected president and chief operating officer and became a member of Sohio's board of directors.

During the first half of the 1980s, Sohio enjoyed the rewards of its investment in Alaska. Our debt-to-total-capital ratio dropped from an unheard of level of 77 percent in 1977 to a much healthier 30 percent as we took steps to strengthen our balance sheet. We became the 15th largest company in America, in terms of assets. Net income increased about twenty-five fold from what we earned before our involvement in Alaska, and cash flow followed suit. Although our stock price appreciated significantly over the same period, its growth was roughly half of that of our net income. This difference was due primarily to the terms of the special stock: the number of common stock equivalencies of BP's special stock increased significantly as crude oil production from our Prudhoe Bay properties increased. This increase in common shares outstanding reduced the growth in our earnings per share, which produced a corresponding drag on the growth of our stock price, relative to the growth in earnings. It also increased BP's ownership in Sohio from about 26 percent at the outset to approximately 55 percent.

Although our improved lot in life was certainly welcome, more than a few major challenges existed. We needed to develop strategic plans for redeploying the substantial sums of cash being generated in Alaska. And we needed to develop an organization capable of managing the enterprise that we had evolved into. Over time, we would essentially double the number of people we employed. Molding them into a lean, mean, well-oiled machine would require the kind of effort that is measured in years.

There was another nettlesome issue on the horizon about which we could do little but watch and wait. BP's situation, vis-à-vis Sohio, was less than desirable. Despite the fact that BP had a majority ownership position, there was a large contingent of public shareholders who held a minority ownership, and the officers and directors of Sohio had a fiduciary duty to do what was right for all of the company's shareholders.

That imperative created a good deal of tension between BP and Sohio, and made it difficult, if not impossible, for BP to realize the advantages that would be available if it owned Sohio outright through consolidating operations, eliminating overhead, etc. Most of Sohio's management team recognized it was only a matter of time before BP would resolve its dilemma by buying out the minority interest. The only questions were when and how.

Sometime during 1985, Sir Peter Walters, BP's chairman and chief executive officer, summoned me to London for a private meeting. He told me that BP had identified only two candidates to succeed him—Bob Horton and David Simon—and BP was desirous of having a third horse in the race. Me. The idea was that I would move to London and become a managing director of BP, and Bob Horton would replace me as president of Sohio. They hadn't quite figured out my responsibilities, except that I wouldn't have anything to do with the Western Hemisphere. I was extremely skeptical for a couple of reasons. First, an American as chairman of BP was highly unlikely. Second, Horton, who I knew well, was a very domineering individual, and I suspected that replacing me with him had more to do with furthering BP's objective of acquiring the minority interest in Sohio they didn't own than it did with adding another contender for Sir Peter's job. I thanked Sir Peter for the opportunity, but declined, saying that I had a lot of unfinished business at Sohio to tend to.

He wasn't happy.

I had always assumed that one day BP would tell us they were going to make a tender offer for the stock they didn't own. When that happened, even though BP eventually would prevail, we would go the mat and wage an aggressive battle to improve the price they were offering. Once the Sohio minority shareholders were bought out and the dust settled, I would be out of a job.

Little did I know that BP had a better idea.

During 1986, the Saudis flooded the market with crude oil, and the price of oil was cut in half from the previous year. This price erosion had a severe impact on our earnings, and that gave BP the opening they were looking for. Citing our disappointing performance and a need for "more confidence" in Sohio's management, BP executives orchestrated a boardroom coup and fired both Al Whitehouse, who had replaced Charlie Spahr as chairman and CEO, and me. Bob Horton was named as Al's replacement.

III

At the time of my unceremonious ouster from Sohio, I had just recently joined the boards of Eaton Corporation and the Federal Reserve Bank of Cleveland. I phoned both to inform them of my change in status and offered my resignation. I'm most grateful neither accepted it. But finding employment as an ex-president of a Fortune 15 company was an exercise in futility. The petroleum industry rarely hires top executives from the outside, preferring to promote from within. And search firms presumed that I would not be interested in taking a position beneath the one I had. That meant, almost certainly, there weren't going to be any offers coming my way. I was left to create my own opportunities.

I launched two start-ups, with modest success. I came to have a great deal of respect for those entrepreneurs who succeed in starting enterprises. It's tough. Following that, I segued into full-time board work, serving from time to time as a director of about a dozen firms—some private, but mostly publicly held.

III

During his first year in office, Horton made a point of emphasizing Sohio's problems as he saw them, and Sohio's stock price decreased further. Then in 1987, BP made a tender offer for the Sohio stock it didn't own. Horton professed to be shocked! He said the situation put him in a serious conflict of interest. He was still an employee of BP, the entity making the tender offer, while at the same time he was the chairman of Sohio, the company under attack. He recused himself from participating in the matter, which meant that no serious opposition to the price being offered would be raised by Sohio's management. In short order, the tender offer was successfully concluded and The Standard Oil Company, founded in Cleveland, Ohio by John D. Rockefeller in 1870, no longer existed.

From time to time, individuals familiar with Sohio's story asked me if Sohio's management would have entered into the amalgamation with BP had we known it would cost us our jobs and that our company would be swallowed up by BP. In *Fortune*'s article on our Alaskan venture, Charlie Spahr was quoted as saying, "We wanted to be remembered as men of courage and judgment, as risk takers on a grand scale." I fully subscribed to that. And more importantly, we were being paid to create value for our shareholders, not entrench ourselves. In that we clearly succeeded. In spades.

And so my answer to the inquiry has always been, "Absolutely!"

36. POST SCRIPTS

T**he Glory Of This House Is Hospitality:** In October 1973, the year following Hospitality's highly successful IPO, the Organization of Arab Petroleum Exporting Countries imposed an embargo on the countries supporting Israel in the Yom Kippur War. In short order, the price of a barrel of crude oil rose from around $3.50 to over $10 and Americans were standing in line to buy gasoline. The conventional wisdom that the US was entering an era of increasing leisure time was replaced by the conventional wisdom that nobody could afford to drive anymore. Florida real estate values cratered, since tourists could no longer get there. Motels became nonessential, and their stock prices tumbled. Hospitality's shares dropped from its initial offering price of $34 per share to $3 and change, and the company's fortunes languished through the 1970s.

The oil industry—Sohio included—took the opportunity to once again remind the American public about the perils of importing increasingly greater amounts of oil from politically unstable parts of the world. I often wondered—if we were so omniscient—why we hadn't warned potential Hospitality investors of the looming threat. Fortunately, none of the plaintiff's bar saw fit to make the case. In the litigious society that exists today, the price erosion experienced by Hospitality's shareholders would have triggered an automatic class action lawsuit, with the courts rewarding the lawyers with munificent sums for their vigilance while shareholders would be given coupons to supersize their order of fries the next time they ate at McDonald's.

Years later, after I became president of Sohio, one of my associates who was affiliated with Hospitality told me that a New York real estate developer wanted to make a tender offer for the publicly traded stock of Hospitality, but would only do so if we would sell him Sohio's 49 percent stake in the company. He wanted to own 100 percent of Hospitality so he could take the company private. The developer let it be known that he was doing this for his wife, who wanted to get into the lodging business. I could understand buying some bling for the little woman for her birthday, but I found this a bit strange and was curious whether the developer was credible and had the wherewithal to pull off the deal. I was assured he was credible. Hospitality was no longer strategic to us and a sale of our interest made sense as long as the price was right. Turns out, the developer was Harry Helmsley, whose wife was the "Queen of Mean" Leona Helmsley.

Mr. Helmsley acquired Hospitality and changed its name to Harley Hotels, a portmanteau of "Harry" and "Helmsley."

III

Winnie Was Right: History repeats itself. Sir Winston Churchill said, "You can always count on the Americans to do the right thing—after they've tried everything else." If he were alive today, my guess is he would change that to— "after they've tried everything else—twice," since what is happening in our country today on the energy front is a repeat of what occurred in the 1970s. Think the Trans Alaska Pipeline vis-à-vis the Keystone Pipeline. Or the US Synthetic Fuels Corporation vis-à-vis Solyndra.

III

Eating Peanuts: During the period of time of heavy expenditures for our Alaskan venture, our participation in the commercial paper markets was so large that our movements alone occasionally masked what was really happening. At the time of the first closing on our $1.75 billion private placement, we had $780 million of commercial paper outstanding, which represented about seven percent of the nonfinancial, dealer-placed paper market of $11.2 billion. With our share of the proceeds from the first tranche of the private placement, we reduced the amount of commercial paper outstanding by $440 million.

In its bulletin published in March 1976, the Federal Reserve said in the fourth quarter of 1975:

> Outstanding nonfinancial commercial paper declined during the quarter, despite a wider spread between the bank prime rate and the commercial paper rate. Because companies with high quality ratings have accounted for most of the borrowings in the commercial paper market since early 1974, the drop in volume suggests that such companies are generating substantial amounts of internal funds to meet current operating needs.

Obviously not the case since we used the proceeds from our debt offering to pay down commercial paper.

The Fed also noted that loan demand during the week of Nov. 15, 1975, dropped by $200 million. During that week, Sohio paid down $175 million of bank loans with proceeds from the private placement, while BP paid down $150 million. Absent the lowering of bank debt that was occasioned by our private placement borrowing rather than cash generated from operations, loan demand actually went up.

III

We Come Cross Big Water in Silver Bird: It would be easy to second guess the original negotiators' decision to hurry up and award a $100 million dollar contract to the Japanese instead of using it as leverage to obtain favorable credit terms. However, the prospect of losing $7 million of tax credits gave them good reason to do that. They were also concerned about getting production of the pipe underway as soon as possible. Little did they know that, as it turned out, manufacturing the pipe was not on the critical path after all. Given the four-year delay in getting the federal right-of-way permit, all 800 miles of the pipe were produced, delivered to Alaska and distributed to a number of large storage areas along the pipeline route, where it sat for a few years before it was actually needed. But considering the inflationary pressures on prices during that period of time, it was probably still a good deal.

III

Pac Tex: After the task of raising the capital necessary for our Alaskan venture was completed, I was moved from vice president of finance and planning to vice president of transportation in February of 1978. My new duties included responsibility for our pipeline and marine interests. As such, I inherited the PacTex project, our proposal to run a pipeline from Long Beach, California to a terminal near Midland, Texas. We only had a small organization in Long Beach, but a lot of good work had been done there in the prior three years. Nonetheless, the requisite approvals had yet to be granted, and much work remained to get them.

One of the early decisions to be made was choosing an agency in California as a "partner" in our permitting efforts. There were several from which to choose. We had retained local counsel with expertise in environmental permitting matters. Our counsel told us that by choosing the right agency, should that agency be sued in an attempt to stop the project—which was certain to happen—and if the opponents won in the lower court—which was highly likely—then the appeal of that decision would go immediately to the Supreme Court of California. Otherwise, the legal battle would slowly wind its way through California's court system before it got to the Supreme Court, costing us precious time. We made the right choice and it worked exactly like we were told it would. The agency we selected was sued. We lost, and we appealed. The case went directly to the Supreme Court of California. The controversial Rose Bird, a Governor Edmund G. "Jerry" Brown Jr. appointee, was the chief justice at that time, and it was up to her to decide when to hear our case. The case didn't come up—for years. It was like it had disappeared into a black hole, and there was no way to pry it loose or to get information on its status from Chief Justice Bird.

While awaiting the resolution of the pending legal challenges, we made some progress on other fronts. As a quid pro quo for the air quality construction permits for the Long Beach terminal, Governor Jerry Brown's administration suggested that Sohio, as a partial trade-off for the emissions at the terminal, install antipollution equipment at a Southern California Edison Company power plant. After almost a year of three-party negotiations, an agreement was reached. Contingent upon our PacTex project going forward, we agreed to pay for the cost of constructing, operating, and maintaining a flue gas scrubber and nitrogen oxide-reducing equipment at one of Edison's power plants. The estimated cost of this was $78 million. On August 18, 1978, in Los Angeles, I signed the agreement and then participated in a news conference with Governor Brown and Howard Allen, executive vice president of Edison, to announce what was described as an historic arrangement. The governor did a great job of extolling the virtues of the transaction he had orchestrated. For his part, Mr. Allen tried to look grateful for being the recipient of Sohio's generosity, knowing full well that if the equipment proved effective, his company would be required to make similar installations at all of its facilities. My assignment was to make sure everybody understood that, while this was an important milestone, a number of additional hurdles had to be cleared before construction of PacTex could begin. That was not a message the governor wanted to be delivered, and as soon as I finished my brief statement, he shut down the news conference, explaining that he had to get to Sacramento for a meeting. His staff prevented reporters from asking me for details about the obstacles that remained. Say what you will about "Governor Moonbeam," he knew how to play the political game.

Amazing how easy it is to throw up roadblocks to progress. The consequences of dong nothing are rarely brought to light, or are as well understood, as the consequences of doing something. A 19 year-old, out-of-work house painter managed to get a referendum on the ballot in Long Beach to prohibit construction of our terminal. If it passed, it would have been the end the project. Our team in Long beach did an excellent job of convincing the community that the project would create jobs and help the local economy. Most importantly, the team convinced Long Beach that the project would improve air quality in the Los Angeles area, not harm it. The referendum was defeated. But that still left us with two major disputes with California, to say nothing of the legal challenges that were still pending.

The Federal Power Commission had years earlier taken under consideration the request by El Paso to abandon its gas transmission line that we wanted to use as part of the PacTex system. But California was opposing this request, claiming it would impair its ability to receive increased supplies of natural gas in the future. This issue between the federal government and California had yet to be resolved some three years later. And after a couple of years of discussions among the Environmental Protection Agency, the California Air Resources Board, and the South Coast Air-Quality Management District, key differences over air quality issues remained unresolved.

Concerned at the seemingly endless delays, I asked for a meeting with our California counsel advising us on legal and environmental matters to update me on our project. I heard nothing encouraging. Then I asked him to tell me, in order to develop our strategy for dealing with obstacles that may lie ahead, what legal maneuvers he would advise the other side to make if he were working for them. He took the bait and began to reel off a series of legal challenges that could delay us for a long, long time. Little did he know that he had just put the kiss of death on PacTex.

PacTex was a different situation than TAPS. Although we endured lengthy delays in getting approvals to start construction of TAPS, we were committed to continuing the struggle for as long as it took for very good reasons. The pipeline was needed to move Prudhoe Bay crude oil to market. Regardless of how far off into the future the start-up of TAPS was pushed, all of the oil produced on the North Slope—some ten billion barrels—would still be shipped through the pipeline.

The rationale for building PacTex was to provide an economic way to deal with the Prudhoe Bay oil that was surplus to the West Coast. Here's the rub. Production from the
Prudhoe Bay field would begin to decline by ten-to-fifteen
percent every year about ten years after startup. Meanwhile,
demand for North Slope crude oil on the West Coast would
increase modestly every year. As a result, at some future
date, the surplus of North Slope crude oil on the West Coast
would disappear, and PacTex would no longer serve a useful
purpose. We estimated this would occur in the early 1990s.
So as getting PacTex into operation was delayed—unlike the
situation with TAPS—its economic life was shortened. Even
using optimistic assumptions about when PacTex approvals
might be granted, we still wouldn't get enough value out of
the system to justify our investment. My next task—not a
pleasant one—would be to recommend shutting down the
project and writing off what we had spent, about $25 mil-
lion. The news was not welcome, but it was understood.

Fortunately, other developments were taking place that
would reduce the cost of the marine alternative to move
the oil surplus to the West Coast market east of the Rockies. A terminal, Petroterminal de Panama, was being built
by Northville Industries on the Pacific side of the Panama
Canal at Charco Azul, which would provide us with a convenient way to transship onto Panamax vessels. Northville
also was planning to build an 80-mile pipeline across the
Isthmus of Panama to the Atlantic where it planned to build
another terminal. Once completed, this system would eliminate the need to move oil through the Panama Canal to get
it to the Gulf Coast or the East Coast of the United States.
Of obvious value to us, we threw our support behind the
project. While waiting for the terminal on the Pacific side of
the canal to be completed, we chartered the British Resolution, a 265,000 dead-weight VLCC (very large crude carrier), from BP, which we anchored off the Bay of Parita to
be used as a "floating" terminal for transshipment purposes.

After five years of futile efforts in California, not a bad
outcome.

III

Full Circle: While I was working my way up the corporate ladder at Sohio, the gentleman who recruited me out of high school to go to the University of Cincinnati and co-op at Lima Refinery, Chuck King, was also advancing through the ranks. When I was elected president of Sohio, Chuck was serving as senior vice president of marketing, refining and employee relations. In my new position, Chuck reported to me.

I believe you should treat everyone with respect. That's especially important in the workplace. There's an old saying "What goes around comes around" and you never know whom you might end up working for. Fortunately, in our case, we had a great relationship and a good deal of mutual respect.

III

The "Halo Effect": Within days after the announcement of my election as president and chief operating officer of The Standard Oil Company, three of the largest Cleveland-based banks invited me to join their boards of directors. I was the same individual the day after my ascension to the president's office as I was the day before. Yet I was being viewed and treated differently. That made a real impression on me, and I learned early in my tenure to draw a distinction between me, the individual, and the aura of the office I occupied. That helped me to stay grounded and avoid getting overly enamored with myself when acclamations I received were destined for whoever sat in the president's chair.

By virtue of my position at Sohio, I became a director of the American Petroleum Institute (API). I was appointed to API's Environmental Liaison Committee, which met every six months with representatives from the environmental community—organizations such as the Sierra Club, Friends of the Earth, and the Wilderness Society. The temperament of these advocacy groups ranged from moderate to extreme. As one of the younger members of the committee, I was asked to foster a relationship with a few of those in the latter category.

Jay D. Hair served as the president and chief executive officer of the National Wildlife Federation from 1981 to 1995, when its membership swelled to 6 million. He was a prominent leader in the environmental community, and we got to know each other through our liaison sessions, and time spent together on field trips the committee members and their counterparts took to environmentally sensitive areas.

Jay called me to discuss an idea he had. He wanted to establish a roundtable composed of environmental advocates and industry representatives to discuss issues of mutual interest in a fashion similar to the API Liaison Committee. The industry representatives would sponsor the effort through annual donations in the neighborhood of $50,000.

I told Jay I thought his idea was an interesting one. Encouraged, he asked, "Would Sohio be willing to be one of the sponsors?"

"I can't speak for Sohio," I said. "Apparently you haven't heard, but I was fired last week."

"You're no longer president of Sohio?" he said.

"No, I'm not," I replied.

"Then why am I talking to you?" he said and hung up the phone.

This encounter with Jay, which I found amusing, jump-started my transition to life after Sohio. Although there were significant adjustments that would take place, my early realization about the halo effect of the office of the president minimized the magnitude of the change.

ABOUT THE AUTHOR

John Miller grew up in Lima, Ohio in a family with long-time, Midwestern roots. He received a degree in chemical engineering with honors in 1960, and an honorary Doctor of Commercial Science in 1983 from the University of Cincinnati. Mr. Miller worked for The Standard Oil Company (Sohio) as a student in the cooperative education program while attending college. Upon graduation, he joined Sohio as a permanent employee and spent the next twenty-six years with that company. During the latter part of his career with Sohio, he served as president, chief operating officer and director of the company.

After leaving Sohio, Mr. Miller founded and served as chairman and CEO of TBN Holdings Inc., a company engaged in resource recovery, and Petroleum Partners Inc., a firm that provided management services to the petroleum industry.

In addition to currently serving as chairman of the boards of Graphic Packaging Holding Company and Cambrex Corporation, Mr. Miller formerly served as chairman of the Federal Reserve Bank of Cleveland. He also served as a director of Eaton Corporation for 25 years, as well as serving on the boards of nine other companies.

Mr. Miller has three grown children, seven grandchildren, and lives with his wife, Karen, in Hunting Valley, Ohio.

ACKNOWLEDGMENTS

There are many people who played a part in making the financing of Sohio's Alaskan venture a success story. First and foremost, Paul Phillips. He was not only a great mentor to me, but we also became good friends. My career at Sohio would not have been nearly as successful absent his help and support, and for that I am forever grateful. Also of particular note are those who served with me in Sohio's Finance Department: Ron McGimpsey, Bala Ganesan, and Bob Shockey; Sohio's Legal Department: George J. Dunn, an exceptional business lawyer, and his able assistant, Karen Shanahan; David Goodman, Morgan Stanley's partner on our account, without whose creativity and diligence, success might have eluded us; Sam F. Pryor III and Jesse Robert Lovejoy of Davis Polk and Wardwell; Morgan Stanley's outside counsel; Sohio's outside counsel, H. James Sheedy of Squire, Sanders & Dempsey; Sohio's external auditors: Emil Guia, Hugh Mullen, Dick Popeney and the supporting cast at accounting firm, Ernst & Ernst. I offer to all of them, as well as many others too numerous to mention individually, my heartfelt thanks for their important contributions to Sohio's transformation.

Too, I'd like to thank Becca Braun who helped me turn my stories into a worthwhile read, and Bruce Akers, an old friend whose constant urgings to write this book caused me to finally get around to it if for no other reason than to get him off my back.